Gaol Experiences of Mahatma Gandhi

Books by the same Author

- Complete Biography of Mahatma Gandhi (The) (In 3 Volumes)
- Gandhi in Modern World
- Inspiring Thoughts of Mahatma Gandhi: Gandhi in Daily Life
- Mahatma Gandhi on Ethics
- Mahatma Gandhi on Sarvodaya
- Mahatma Gandhi on Untouchability
- Mahatma Gandhi Speaks: Selected Speeches and Writings
- Revising HIND SWARAJ
- Understanding Gandhi: Speeches and Writings That Reveal His Mind, Methods and Mission
- World Crisis and the Gandhi Way
- Mahatma Gandhi on Health
- Gandhi and Nehru: Reflections Through Letters

About the Author

Anil Dutta Mishra is a distinguished Gandhian scholar and writer. He started his career as Assistant Professor in the Department of Non-violence and Peace Studies, Jain Vishva Bharati University, Ladnun, Rajasthan, became Deputy Director of National Gandhi Museum and Honourary Professor, Centre for Gandhian Philosophy and Human Development, Gayatri Vidya Parishad Degree College [Autonomous], Visakhapatnam.
Mishra has held the post of General Secretary of Indian Society of Gandhian Studies, Alliance for Sarvodaya, Member Board of Studies, Nagpur and Punjab Universities and is Member of Gandhian Studies Centre of different colleges and universities across India sponsored by UGC and presently Honourary Treasurer, IIPA Delhi Regional Branch. He has authored/edited 30 books and published a number of research papers. His recent book *Reading Gandhi* is widely acclaimed.
Email: anilduttamishra@gmail.com

GAOL EXPERIENCES OF MAHATMA GANDHI

Anil Dutta Mishra

CONCEPT PUBLISHING COMPANY PVT. LTD.
NEW DELHI-110059

ISBN-13: 978-93-5125-246-7

First Published 2016

Published and Printed by

Since 1974

Concept Publishing Company Pvt. Ltd.
Regd. Office:
A/15-16, Commercial Block, Mohan Garden,
New Delhi-110059 (INDIA)
Phones : 25351460, 25351794,
Fax : 091-11-25357109
Email : publishing@conceptpub.com
Website: www.conceptpub.com

Editorial Office: H-13, Bali Nagar, New Delhi-110 015, India.

Cataloging in Publication Data—DK Courtesy: D.K. Agencies (P) Ltd. <docinfo@dkagencies.com>

Gandhi, *Mahatma,* 1869-1948., **author.**

Gaol experiences of Mahatma Gandhi / [translator], Anil Dutta Mishra.
pages cm
Translated from Gujarati.
Articles previously published in Indian opinion and Young India.
Includes index.
ISBN 9789351252467

1. Gandhi, Mahatma, 1869-1948—Imprisonment. 2. Statesmen—India—Biography. 3. Political prisoners—India—Biography. I. Mishra, Anil Dutta, 1965- translator. II. Title.

DS481.G3A3 2016 DDC 954.035092 23

Preface

Man makes his own history and destiny but not as he wishes. In the case of Gandhi this was proved to be wrong. Gandhi was the real author of his destiny. One step at a time in right direction is enough for determined Gandhi to achieve his goal. He overcomes all the human weakness through vows and determination and never repeated the mistakes. For Gandhi, learning is a lifelong process and one can learn at any age, any time and any place. He was a learner through his life. He was in search of Truths. His life was an experiment of Truths. He was travelling from one truth to another truth to reach the final Truth.

Gandhi a true *Karamyogi* used every odd opportunity as a new beginning and blessing for life. Converting negative into positive was a way of life for Gandhi. He believes in beauty of compromise but never compromise on issue which is unethical and undermines the integrity, self-interest and principles. Gandhi's concern were contemporary but its impact was timeless. Step-by-step, through hard work and determination he became mass leader and voice of voiceless. Finally, he became *Mahatma* and undisputed leader of India.

Gandhi spend more than a half decay in various goals in South Africa and India. Lord Krishna born in prison and liberated his parents from Kansh. Gave gyan to Arjun in form of Gita. Bal Gandadhar Tilak wrote Geetarahasya while he was in Mandalay prison. Pandit Jawaharlal Nehru wrote 'An Autobiography', 'Discovery of India', and 'Glimpses of World History' in prison. Gandhi also wrote discourse on Gita in prison. These great people converted the darkness of prison life into the pearl of wisdom by their creative work when will remain a guiding force for future generations. They used their prison life to further strengthen the freedom struggle through their academic works.

To make the book reader friendly it has been divided into three parts. In all the three parts Gandhi's original writings entitled 'My Gaol Experiences', My Second Experience in Gaol', 'My Third Experiences in Gaol' and 'My Jail Experiences' are placed for reader's deeper understnding of the subject.

I am sure that the book 'Gaol Experiences of Mahatma Gandhi' will open new vistas of research and proper understanding of Gandhi on this issue.

In writing this book I had received, over the years, very valuable help from friends, teachers and colleagues. I am grateful to them. My family has always stood behind me in all my academic endeavours. My wife, Dr. Sweta Mishra, Associate Professor, Department of Political Science, Gargi College, University of Delhi, went through the final draft and provided her valuable inputs.

Last but not the least, I am grateful to Shri Ashok Kumar Mittal of Concept Publishing Company Pvt. Ltd., New Delhi, for bringing out this book in present form and that too within record time.

Anil Dutta Mishra
anilduttamishra@gmail.com

Contents

Part One

MY GAOL EXPERIENCES

1
My Gaol Experiences–I[1]

Many friends have asked me to reduce to writing my experiences of the gaol life, all too brief though it was. There were certain things that came under my observation which might be of advantage if they were put in a more or less permanent form. Believing as I do firmly that incarceration may often be the means of opening the gateway to freedom, liberty, and reform, the experiences I am about to relate may not be profitless to those who do not mind, for the sake of a principle, suffering some inconvenience, or, at any rate, restraint on their personal liberty.

It was on the 10th of January, 1908, in the afternoon of a Friday, that Messrs P.K. Naidoo, C.M. Pillay, Karwa, Easton and Fortoen (the latter two Chinese) and I were sentenced to be imprisoned for two months, without hard labour, for the crime of not having taken out our registration certificates under the Asiatic Law Amendment Act[2]. I was the first to be tried at Johannesburg, and, after receiving my sentence, and after having been detained for a few minutes at the prisoners' yard attached to the Magistrate's Court, I was asked to get into a cab, to which I was stealthily taken in order to evade the enormous crowd that was waiting outside the Court House, and was quickly driven to the Fort. Many were the thoughts that came surging through my mind as I was being driven. Was I to be specially treated as a purely political prisoner? Was I to be separated from my fellow-prisoners? Was I to be taken to the Johannesburg gaol at all? To my very great relief I was soon disillusioned. I was not to be separated from Mr. Naidoo and others who were tried with me, nor were we to receive any special treatment. At the same time I was a little unprepared for what followed. We were all first taken to the reception room, as the room which is used for measuring and dressing prisoners is called.

There we were weighed and totally undressed. We were given non-labour clothes to wear, consisting of trousers, shirt, jumper, cap, socks, and a pair of closed *sandals*. We were all required to give our digit impressions, and at about four O'clock marched to our cell with eight ounces of bread for our evening meal.

CLASSIFICATION OF ASIATICS WITH NATIVES

The cell was situated in the Native quarters and we were housed in one that was labelled "For Coloured Debtors". It was this experience for which we were perhaps all unprepared. We had fondly imagined that we would have suitable quarters apart from the Natives.

As it was, perhaps, it was well that we were classed with the Natives. We would now be able to study the life of Native prisoners, their customs and manners. I felt, too, that passive resistance had not been undertaken too soon by the Indian community. Degradation underlay the classing of Indians with Natives. The Asiatic Act seemed to me to be the summit of our degradation. It did appear to me, as I think it would appear to any unprejudiced reader, that it would have been simple humanity if we were given special quarters. The fault did not lie with the gaol authorities. It was the fault of the law that has made no provision for the special treatment of Asiatic prisoners. Indeed, the Governor of the gaol tried to make us as comfortable as he could within the regulations. The chief warder, as also the head warder, who was in immediate charge of us, completely fell in with the spirit that actuated the Governor. But he was powerless to accommodate us beyond the horrible din and the yells of the Native prisoners throughout the day and partly at night also. Many of the Native prisoners are only one degree removed from the animal and often created rows and fought among themselves in their cells. The Governor could not separate the very few Indian prisoners (It speaks volumes for Indians that among several hundred there were hardly half a dozen Indian prisoners.) from the cells occupied by the Native prisoners. And yet it is quite clear that separation is a physical necessity. So, much was the classification of Indians and other Asiatics with the Natives insisted upon that our jumpers, which being new were not fully marked, had to be labelled "N", meaning Natives. How this thoughtless classification has resulted in the Indians being partly starved will be clearer when we come to consider the question of food.

DESCRIPTION OF THE CELL

The cell in which we were placed was legally capable of holding thirteen prisoners, so that there was, naturally, sufficient accommodation to start with. It was a novel sensation to be locked up at halfpast five. The cell was a galvanized-iron construction, fairly strong, though none too strong for prisoners bent on escaping. There was, perhaps, fair ventilation. But two small windows at the top, half open, and apertures in the opposite wall hardly reach modern requirements, though I was assured that these cells were the best ventilated of all the prisons in the Transvaal. There was electric light in the cell, but the only lamp in it was not strong enough to do any reading with any degree of comfort. The light was switched off at eight O'clock in the evening and was spasmodically switched on and off during the night.

A bucket of water and a tin tumbler was our ration of water for the night. For natural convenience a bucket in a tray with disinfectant fluid in it was placed in a corner. Our bedding consisted of wooden planks fixed to three-inch legs, two blankets, an apology for a pillow, and matting. At our request the Governor ordered a table and two benches to be placed in the room for writing purposes.

The Meals

The cell was opened at six O'clock, and with the day began our first meal. For the first week we were served with twelve ounces of mealie pap. Most of us had more of the spoon than of the porridge for the first breakfast. Neither the Chinese nor the Indians were at all in the habit of taking mealic porridge, especially as it was without any milk or sugar. The following is the scale for non-labour Native prisoners for the first week: breakfast daily, twelve ounces of mealie porridge; dinner, Monday, Wednesday and Friday, twelve ounces of beans; Tuesday, Thursday, Saturday and Sunday, one quart of mealie porridge; supper daily, four ounces of crushed mealies and one ounce of fat. Indian prisoners, however, get instead of crushed mealies, four ounces of rice and one ounce of ghee (clarified butter). This diet was hardly satisfactory not because it was not palatable but because it was not a diet at all suitable for the Asiatic Constitution. The Chinese fared worse because they had the entire Native scale and therefore no rice.

For the first few days, for most of us, it meant practically starvation. Even when we got over the natural repugnance, it was a diet that constipated some of us and gave diarrhoea to the others; but we were determined to go through it and not to ask for any favours or concessions. We felt that it was for the Governor to move and see that a more suitable diet was issued to us. When, therefore, the Governor enquired whether we had anything to say regarding diet, we simply stated that we did not wish to ask for any concessions, though the diet was not suitable. For the second week the scale was a little relieved by the addition of eight ounces of potatoes or vegetables to the dinner when it consisted of mealie porridge, and on Sunday twelve ounces of meat were also added; but, as most of us were either vegetarians or could not take the meat as it was not religiously cut, we had one pound of vegetables. This diet, however, did not last long.

Indian Opinion, 7-3-1908

NOTES

1. This appeared in two instalments in the English section under Gandhiji's name as "Special to *Indian Opinion*".
2. Asiatic Registration Act.

2
My Experience in Gaol–II[1]

Though the imprisonment that the Indian [Satyagrahis] and I suffered for a righteous cause was all too brief, I propose to describe my gaol experiences in these columns, having been asked to do so by a number of persons. Also, I think it may be useful to others. It is also my belief that there are many [other] rights that the Indian community is yet to win by courting imprisonment. It is, therefore, necessary for everyone to have an idea of the hardships of gaol life.

Often we imagine hardships where in fact there are none. Clearly, nothing but good can result from a knowledge of the true state of affairs.

After two [earlier] attempts by the Government to arrest and imprison me it happened at last at 2 p.m. on January 10. Before my colleagues and I received our sentences a telegram was received from Pretoria, which reported that the Indians arrested there for not complying with the Act had received [sentences of] three months' hard labour and fines in addition, with a further term of three months' hard labour in default of payment. I was upset by the news, and asked the Magistrate to give me the maximum penalty, but this was not done.[2]

And so we were all awarded two months' simple imprisonment each. Messrs P.K. Naidoo, C.M. Pillay, Karwa, Easton and Fortoen were my fellow-prisoners. The two last named are from China. After the sentence I was detained for a few minutes in the Prisoners' Yard behind the Court. Then I was secretly led to a cab. Many were the thoughts that surged in my mind. Was I to be given a separate cell and treated as a political prisoner? Was I to be isolated from my fellow prisoners?

Was I to be taken out of Johannesburg? These were the thoughts running through my mind. I was accompanied by a detective, who was apologetic. I told him that he had no reason to be, as he was only doing his duty in taking me to gaol.

All that I had imagined was soon falsified. I was taken to where all prisoners are kept, and was soon joined by my fellow-prisoners. First, all of us were weighed. Then we were asked to give our finger-impressions. After being stripped we were given prison uniforms to wear, consisting of black trousers, a shirt, a jumper, a cap and socks. We were given a bag each to pack away our own clothes in. Before being led off to our ward, we were each given eight ounces of bread. We were then marched off to a prison intended for Kaffirs.

INDIANS ON PAR WITH KAFFIRS

There, our garments were stamped with the letter "N", which meant that we were being classed with the Natives. We were all prepared for hardships, but not quite for this experience. We could understand not being classed with the whites, but to be placed on the same level with the Natives seemed too much to put up with. I then felt that Indians had not launched on passive resistance too soon. Here was further proof that the obnoxious law was intended to emasculate the Indians.

It was, however, as well that we were classed with the Natives. It was a welcome opportunity to study the treatment meted out to Natives, their conditions [of life in gaol] and their habits. Looked at from another point of view, it did not seem right to feel bad about being bracketed with them. At the same time, it is indubitably right that Indians should have separate cells. The cells for Kaffirs were adjacent to ours. They used to make a frightful din in their cells as also in the adjoining yard. We were given a separate ward because we were sentenced to simple imprisonment; otherwise we would have been in the same ward [with the Kaffirs]. Indians sentenced to hard labour are in fact kept with the Kaffirs.

Apart from whether or not this implies degradation, I must say it is rather dangerous. Kaffirs are as a rule uncivilised—the convicts even more so. They are troublesome, very dirty and live almost like animals. Each ward contains nearly 50 to 60 of them. They often started rows and fought among themselves. The reader can easily imagine the plight of the poor Indian thrown into such company!

OTHER INDIAN PRISONERS

Apart from us, there were hardly three or four Indian prisoners in the whole gaol. They were locked up with the Kaffirs and, to that extent, they were worse off than we. However, I noticed that they were quite cheerful and enjoyed better health than when they were outside. They had earned the favour of the Chief Warder. Being quick at their work and well informed, as compared with the Kaffirs, they were given respectable work to do inside the gaol. That is, they supervised the work on the machines in the store or did similar jobs which were not strenuous or did not seem unclean. They were particularly helpful to us.

WARD

We were kept in a ward[3] which had room for 13 persons. It was labelled "For Coloured Debtors"; that is, for the most part it was used for Coloured persons who were imprisoned for civil offences. For ventilation, the ward had two small windows with a strong iron grilling which, I thought, did not let in enough air. Galvanized iron sheets served for walls with glazed apertures at three places, half an inch in diameter, through which the gaolers could watch the prisoners while remaining unobserved themselves. The ward next to ours had Kaffir prisoners in it. In the wards beyond, there were Kaffirs, Chinese and Cape Boys—all witnesses—who had been locked up in gaol lest they should abscond.

[From Gujarati]

Indian Opinion, 7-3-1908

NOTES

1. This and the subsequent articles in this series were published as "From Mr. Gandhi".
2. *Vide* "Trial at Johannesburg", 10-1-1908.
3. It is not clear whether ÀùËÍí, used in this series of articles, refers, in any given context, to a cell or a ward. It would, however, appear that the *Satyagrahis*, about 50 of them, were lodged together in a large room.

3
My Experience in Gaol–III

In front of the cell [s] there was a small yard in which we could move about during the day. It was [however] too small for the purpose. There is a rule that prisoners in this ward may not go out of the enclosed space without permission, since the bath, urinals and latrines are all located within the yard. For bathing there were two large stone basins and two spouts which served for a shower. There were buckets for defecation and two more for urine. There was no provision for privacy in the bath or latrine. Also, the Gaol Regulations forbade the provision of separate latrines which would allow the prisoners privacy. It often happened, therefore, that two or three prisoners sat down in a row. The arrangements for bathing were similar. The buckets for urine, too, stood in the open. This may well cause a feeling of revulsion; some would be offended by it. But on reflection one realizes that a gaol cannot provide for privacy and that no feeling of shame should attach to the performing of these functions in public. It is, therefore, necessary patiently to form the required habits without being squeamish or annoyed at the public nature of these arrangements.

For sleeping, there were hard wooden planks [mounted on] legs only three inches high. Each prisoner had two rugs, a small pillow and a coir mat large enough to roll them up in. Sometimes three rugs were allowed to a prisoner but only as a favour. Some were put out at the thought of [sleeping on] a hard bench. Those used to soft mattresses cannot easily take to hard bedding. According to medical science, hard bedding is to be preferred. If we, therefore, adopt the practice of using hard bedding at home, we will not find it difficult to get used to the kind of bedding available in gaol. A bucket of water was provided in the cell, and another bucket placed on a large tray served for a chamber-pot, for no prisoner was allowed to leave the cell at night.

Everyone was provided, according to his needs, with a little soap, a homespun towel and a wooden spoon.

SANITATION

I must say that sanitation in the gaol was excellent. Everyday, the floor of the cell was washed with a disinfectant and the edges of the floor [skirting the wall] lime-washed. The cell therefore, always looked fresh. The bathroom and the commodes were also washed with soap and disinfectant. I believe, I am myself very particular about sanitation. Therefore, when, towards the end, a large number of our people joined us, I myself used to wash the commodes with disinfectant fluid. To remove the stool, a few Chinese prisoners turned up every morning at nine O'clock. Afterwards, whenever it was necessary to clean up or wash, we had to do it ourselves. The planks of the beds were washed everyday with sand and water. The only inconvenience was that, as it happened, the pillows and rugs changed hands among the hundreds of prisoners. Though, there was a rule that required the rugs to be aired in the sun everyday, it was hardly ever observed.

SOME RULES

There are some gaol rules which everyone should know. The prisoners are locked up at half-past five in the afternoon. They read or converse in the cell up to eight in the evening. At eight, everyone must go to bed, meaning that even if one cannot sleep, one must get into bed. Talking among prisoners after eight constitutes a breach of Gaol Regulations. The Kaffir prisoners do not observe this rule too strictly. The warders on night duty, therefore, try to silence them by knocking against the walls with their truncheons and shouting, *"Thula! thula!"* Prisoners are strictly forbidden to smoke—a rule which is enforced scrupulously. But I saw that the confirmed smokers among the prisoners broke the rule on the sly. A bell is rung at half-past five in the morning to wake up the prisoners. Everyone must then get up, roll up his bedding and wash. The door of the cell is opened at six when each prisoner must stand up with his arms crossed and his bedding rolled up beside him. A sentry then calls the roll. By a similar rule, every prisoner is required to stand beside his bed, while he is being locked up [at night]. The prisoners may not have anything else in their possession except what is given them by the gaol authorities.

Except clothes, they are forbidden to keep anything without the Governor's permission. One of the buttons on every prisoner's shirt has sewn on to it a small pocket which contains a card bearing his number, his name, the particulars of his sentence, etc. Normally, the prisoners may not stay in the cell during the day. Those sentenced to hard labour cannot do so in any case, since they are engaged in their work, but even the others are not allowed to stay in. They must remain in the yard outside the cell. The Governor had allowed us a table and two benches in the ward, and these were very useful.

There is a rule that every prisoner sentenced to two months [or more] must have his hair cropped close and the moustache shaved off.

In the case of Indians the rule is not enforced rigorously. Should a prisoner object, his moustache is spared? In this connection I had an amusing experience. I knew very well that prisoners had to have their hair cropped. I also knew that the rule about having the prisoner's hair and moustache removed was really for his own convenience and not to humiliate him. Personally, I believe that it is a very useful rule.

In gaol there are no combs or other means for keeping the hair tidy. If the hair is not groomed, there is the risk of scabies. On hot days, hair makes one feel extremely uncomfortable. Moreover, the prisoners are not given a looking-glass. There is the danger, therefore, of the moustache remaining unclean. As there is no serviette for use at meals and the wooden spoon is rather awkward to handle, food is apt to stick in the moustache. It was my intention to go through all the experiences of a prisoner. I, therefore, asked the Chief Warder to have my hair cropped and my moustache shaved off. He told me the Governor had strictly forbidden that. I said, I knew that he did not wish to force me [to observe this rule], but that I myself wanted it. He suggested that I might apply to the Governor. The next day, permission was received from him. But he said that, since two days out of my two-month period had elapsed, he had now no right to order the cropping of my hair and moustache. I said, I knew the rule but wanted this of my own free will and for my own convenience. He smilingly demurred. I learnt later that the Governor had felt a little apprehensive. So, I offered to state in writing that I had myself requested the cropping [of my hair]. This allayed the Governor's suspicion, and he ordered the Chief Warder to give me clippers and a pair of scissors. My fellow prisoner, Mr. P. K. Naidoo, was a master of the tonsorial art. I, too, know something of it. When the others saw me cropping my hair and moustache, they saw the point of it, and followed suit. Some of them had only their hair cropped. Mr. Naidoo and I, between us, spent two hours each day clipping the Indians' hair. I believe, this made for better health and convenience. The prisoners looked the smarter for it.

The use of the razor is strictly forbidden in gaol. Only clippers and scissors are allowed.

INSPECTION

When the officials come to inspect the prisoners, the latter have all to line up. As the official approaches, they must take off their caps and salute him. All the prisoners wore caps, and it was not difficult to take them off, for there was a rule that they must be taken off, and this was only proper. The order to line up was given by shouting the command "fall in" whenever an official came. The words "fall in" therefore became our daily diet. They meant that the prisoners should fall in line and stand to attention. This happened four or five times a day. One of these officials, who bore the designation of Assistant Chief Warder, was somewhat strict. The Indian prisoners therefore nicknamed him "General Smuts". He often came early in the morning, and sometimes in the afternoon as well. The doctor came at half-past nine. He appeared to be a kind and well-meaning person. He made solicitous inquiries about our health. Under the Gaol Regulations, every prisoner must undress himself in public for examination by the doctor. But the doctor did not insist on the observance of this rule. Moreover, when the number of Indian prisoners increased, he asked them if anyone had eczema or similar infection, so that he might examine the person in private. The Governor and the Chief Warder used to come at half-past ten or eleven. The Governor appeared to be firm, fair-minded and quiet-tempered. He always had the same questions to ask: "Are you all well? Is there anything you want? Have you any complaints?"

He listened to a request or a complaint patiently and granted every request which was reasonable; if there was a [genuine] grievance, he set matters right. I shall discuss some of the complaints and demands later. The Deputy Governor also came sometimes. He, too, was a kindly person. But the kindest among them all, the most gentle and sympathetic, was the official known as the Chief Warder, who was especially charged with looking after us. He is a very devout man; we were not the only ones to whom he was nice and courteous in every way; [for] the other prisoners were also very warm in their praises of him. He was anxious to respect prisoners' rights. He would condone any minor offence on their part. He was particularly kind to us because he thought that we had not really committed any offence. Often he talked with us and even expressed sympathy.

PRISONERS INCREASE

I mentioned earlier that we were five *Satyagrahi* prisoners to begin with. On Tuesday, January 14, we were joined by Mr. Thambi Naidoo, the Chief Picket, and Mr. Quinn, Chairman of the Chinese Association. All of us were happy to see them. On January 16, 14 others came, Samunder Khan being one of them. He had been sentenced to a two-month term. The remaining 13 included Madrasis, Kanamias and Gujarati Hindus. All of them had been arrested for hawking without licences and fined £2 each with 14 days' imprisonment in default of payment. They had had courage enough to refuse payment of the fine and to prefer imprisonment. On Tuesday, January 21, another 76 persons joined us. Among them, only Nawab Khan had been sentenced to two months, the rest having been fined £2 each with 14 days' imprisonment in default of payment. Most of them were Gujarati Hindus, the rest Kanamias and Madrasis. On Wednesday, January 22, there was a further addition of

35 persons. On the 23rd, three more arrived, one on the 24th, two on the 25th, six on the 28th, and, on the evening of the same day, four more. On the 29th, there were again four arrivals, all of them Kanamias. That made a total of 155 up to January 29. On Thursday, that is, on the 30th, I was taken to Pretoria. But I remember, on that day also, five or six more prisoners arrived.

[From Gujarati]

Indian Opinion, 14-3-1908

4
My Gaol Experiences–IV

CHANGE IN THE DIET

On the 14th of January came Messrs Thambi Naidoo and Quinn. That, however, did not affect the situation much, as they were quite willing to rough it, but on the 18th, fourteen more came. With the exception of one, these were hawkers who were sentenced to pay two pounds fine or to suffer fourteen days' imprisonment. It was not possible to expect these men to accommodate themselves all of a sudden to a diet to which they were never used. Consequently, it was a matter of grave anxiety. It was duly brought to the notice of the Governor who professed helplessness by regulation. He was quite willing to respect any religious objections but where it was a matter merely of likes and dislikes, he could not help. Prison life was prison life and people's tastes could not be respected. All this would be true, if it were merely a matter of tastes. Unfortunately, it was a matter of habit. And the scale having been fixed without due regard for national habits of Asiatics, the system broke down under the stress. just as it would be foolish for Indians to expect national food adjuncts, such as curries, etc., it was foolish for the authorities to have prescribed a diet—however nutritious it might be medically that was unsuitable for Indians. Boiled beef or mutton would be just as useless for Indians as mealie pap. They could live on wheaten and rice preparations, no matter how simple they might be. But they could not live on what might be African delicacies. So that, the new batch of prisoners faced starvation. They went without breakfast. And rice they received for dinner, i.e., four ounces with one ounce of ghee insufficient as it was even with the breakfast was much more so for people who broke their fast on the above quantity of rice.

A PETITION IN PRISON

The following petition[1] was, therefore, forwarded through the Governor to the Director of Prisons.

Owing to the arrival, as stated at the foot of the petition, of about seventy more passive resisters, I requested the Governor either to telegraph or to telephone its contents and to apply for prompt instructions.

This he kindly did and orders were given immediately, pending further consideration, to replace mealie pap for breakfast by four ounces of bread and to do the same thing for supper by issuing eight ounces of bread. Whilst the matter was being further considered, the compromise supervened and we were all discharged.

A CONTRAST

Yet it must be clear to the reader that this question of food for Asiatic Prisoners is too important to be given up. It is only because there are ordinarily very few Indian prisoners in the Transvaal gaols that the matter has not attracted attention before now. The change ordered by the Director removed the most four ounces of bread even for non-labour Prisoners is a mere morsel. And although the medical officer stated that the addition of cocoa or butter or *dholl* would be considered a relish and therefore not allowed as a prison diet, I venture to think that some such addition is absolutely necessary to make bread eatable. Now let us for a moment glance at the scale for non-labour European Prisoners. They get for breakfast one pint of porridge and four ounces of bread; for dinner eight ounces of bread daily, together with meat or soup or beans, potatoes or vegetables; for supper they get eight ounces of bread and one pint of porridge. I understand that they also get cocoa or some such drink. Now it does not seem clear why the Europeans should get porridge *and* four ounces of bread whereas Indians should get four ounces of bread *in place of* porridge. Have the former a greater appetite than Indians?

Then again, why should Indians get only twelve ounces of beans when Europeans get the same quantity of beans and eight ounces of bread?

This is an anomaly which is most difficult to understand. It may be possible to reconcile oneself to the Europeans getting a greater variety of superior or more expensive food; but it is not possible to do so with regard to the quantity of foods. It is obvious, therefore, that the Indian dietary needs a great deal of modification. Then again, the fact that the Colonial Secretary never troubled himself about the food provided for men who could not be classed as ordinary Prisoners betray in my opinion callous contempt for the Indian community. In vie of the compromise effected, one does not wish to say much on this Painful phase of the question.

Indian Opinion, 21-3-1908

NOTE

1. For the text, *vide* "Petition to Director of Prisons", 21-1-1908.

5

My Experience in Gaol–V

Diet is a subject which most of us have to think about some time or other in our lives. In particular, prisoners' food requires the most careful consideration. Their well-being depends a great deal on a good diet. The rule about food in gaol is that one must accept what is offered and take nothing from any other source. Soldiers, too, must eat what is given them. But there is a great difference between soldiers and prisoners. Friends may send gifts of food to soldiers, which they may accept. Prisoners, on the other hand, are forbidden to accept [gifts of] food. Difficulty in regard to food is one important feature of prison life. Even in casual conversation we hear gaol authorities saying that there can be no question of preferences in gaol. When I met the gaol doctor, I asked that bread should be served with tea or ghee. He replied: "You want to indulge your taste. That is not possible in gaol."

Let us now consider the regulation of food in gaol. Indians get the following items of food during the first week: in the morning, twelve ounces of mealie pap without sugar or ghee; for the mid-day meal, four ounces of rice with an ounce of ghee; in the evening, twelve ounces of mealie pap on four days and boiled beans with salt on three days.

This scale is drawn up on the basis of what the Kaffir prisoners get, with this difference that the Kaffirs are given pounded maize and fat in the evening, instead of which Indians get rice [for their mid-day meal]. From the second week onward, along with mealie meal, they get boiled potatoes on two days and vegetables, such as cabbage, pumpkin, on the other two. To those who eat it, meat is also served with vegetables every Sunday from the second week onward.

The prisoners who were the first to arrive had decided not to ask for any favours from the Government but to make do with whatever food was allowed them, provided it was acceptable [from the religious standpoint]. In point of fact, the scale described above was neither adequate for Indians nor suited to them. It may be that dietetically the food was sufficiently nutritious. Mealie meal is the staple of Kaffir diet, so that this scale suits them very well and they thrive on it. But nothing except rice is acceptable to Indians; hardly any of them eat mealie pap. Indians are not used to eating beans as a course in itself and do not find the vegetarian dishes [cooked in gaol] agreeable. The vegetables are not washed, neither are they dressed with spices.

Moreover, the vegetables served to the Kaffir prisoners consist mostly of the leftovers and peelings from the vegetables cooked for the whites. Nothing except salt is allowed by way of condiment. Of sugar one may not even dream. Everyone was therefore bothered by the problem of food. Even so, we the 35 Satyagrahis resolved that the we should not ask for anything from the gaol authorities nor seek a favour. So, we carried on with the food described above.

When the Governor enquired [about the amenities], we told him that our food was unsatisfactory, but that we did not wish to ask for a favour from the Government. It was for the Government to consider whether they should make changes. Otherwise, we would make do with whatever the regulations allowed.

This attitude could not be kept up for long. When others joined us, we agreed that it would not be proper for us to compel them to accept this inconvenience as we did. That they had come to gaol was [sacrifice] enough. It would be proper, we thought, to demand from the Government special treatment for these people. To that end we broached the subject with the Governor. We told him that, though we accepted whatever was given to us, those who came after us would not be able to do so. The Governor thought the matter over and answered that he could [permit] cooking to meet any religious scruples, but that the food itself should remain the same. It was not within his power to effect any changes in it.

Meanwhile, as mentioned earlier,[1] 14 other Indians joined us. Some of them plainly refused to eat mealie pap. They starved. I went through the gaol regulations, and discovered that a petition on this subject could be addressed to the Director of Prisons. We therefore, asked for the Governor's permission to address a petition, and the following petition[2] was forwarded.

This petition was signed by 21 of us. After it had been signed and was about to be submitted, we were joined by another 76 Indians, who also disliked mealie pap. We therefore, added at the end of the petition that the 76 persons do had come in also felt the same difficulty, and that immediate orders should therefore be issued. I requested the Governor to telegraph the contents of this petition. He consented and, after obtaining the permission of the Director on telephone, ordered mealie pap to be replaced by four ounces of bread [for each prisoner]. All of us were happy. From the 22nd, therefore, we got four ounces of bread in the morning, as also in the evening, [that is,] on mealie-pap days. In the evening eight ounces of bread was provided, that is, half a loaf. This arrangement was only provisional, pending further orders. The Governor had meanwhile appointed a committee to go into this question. In the end, it was proposed to allow us flour, ghee, rice and pulses. Nothing further happened and we were released soon after.

When, in the beginning, we were only eight, none of us did any cooking. The rice was not well cooked and in their turn, the green vegetables, too, were cooked badly. Therefore, we also obtained permission to cook our own meals. On the first day, Mr. Karwa offered to cook. He was then replaced by Mr. Thambi Naidoo and Mr. Jivan.

During the last few days they cooked for 150 persons and had to cook once a day. Two days in the week, however, that is, on the green vegetable days, they had to go twice a day [to cook]. Mr. Thambi Naidoo did an admirable job of work, and I looked after the serving.

The readers will observe from the foregoing petition that it is drafted so as to present a case not for preferential treatment for ourselves alone, but for a modification of the food scale for all Indian prisoners. It was in the same light that the matter was placed before the Governor, and he concurred. There is still hope that the ration for Indian prisoners in gaols will be modified.

Moreover, the three Chinese were given something else in place of the rice that we got and were thus the only ones to be refused rice.

This caused some heart-burning. It appeared as though the Chinese were being discriminated against as a class inferior to us. I, therefore, wrote out a petition[3] on their behalf to the Governor and to Mr. Playford. The order was finally passed that the Chinese should get the same food as the Indians.

While on the subject of food, it will be instructive to compare [the Indian] with the European scale. For breakfast, they get porridge with eight ounces of bread. For dinner, again, bread, together with *soup* or meat with potatoes or green vegetables, and for supper, bread and porridge. That is, Europeans get bread thrice a day, so that it makes no difference whether or not they get porridge. Moreover, they are served either meat or soup as an additional item everyday. Over and above these they are given tea or cocoa every afternoon. It is thus clear that both Kaffirs and Europeans get food suited to their tastes.

The poor Indians—nobody bothers about them! They cannot get the food they want. If they are given European diet, the whites will feel insulted. In any case, why should the gaol authorities bother to find out the normal Indian fare? There is nothing for it but to let ourselves be classed with the Kaffirs and starve.

That this state of affairs has gone on till today points, in my view, to a deficiency in our *Satyagraha*. Some Indian prisoners get extra food from without surreptitiously. They, therefore, suffer no inconvenience on this account. There are other Indian prisoners who make do with whatever they are given, and [afterwards] feel ashamed of mentioning their misfortunes or do not care enough for others [to take up the issue]. People outside remain in the dark [about what happens in gaol]. If we were all devoted to truth and remonstrated whenever, there was injustice, we would never have to suffer these inconveniences. If we think more of others than of ourselves, it will be easy to find solutions for these problems.

If it is necessary to find remedies for these problems, it is also necessary to bear another consideration in mind. A prisoner must submit to certain hardships. If there were no hardships, what would be the point of being imprisoned? Those who can control their minds can find happiness even amidst hardships and enjoy being in gaol.

Such persons, however, will not forget the hardships [of gaol life], and, for the sake of others, they ought not to. Moreover, we should give up clinging so tenaciously to our customs and habits. Everyone has heard of the saying, "As the country, so the attire". Since we live in South Africa we must accustom ourselves to whatever is wholesome in the food of the people here. Mealie pap, like wheat, is good, simple and cheap food. Neither can it be said to be tasteless. In fact, for some purposes, mealie pap is better than wheat. I also believe that, out of regard for the country in which we live, we must accept the food grown in the soil of that country, provided of course it is not unwholesome.

Many whites have mealie pap for breakfast every day because they like it. With milk, sugar or ghee, it can be made palatable. Bearing these considerations in mind, and also because there may be many occasions yet for us to go to gaol, we should all get used to mealie pap. If we do that, eating mealie pap with only salt will not appear so much of an ordeal. There are some habits of ours which we must not hesitate to give up in the interests of our country. The nations which have progressed are those which have given in on inessential matters. The members of the Salvation Army win over the hearts of the people among whom they work by adopting their customs, dress, etc.

[From Gujarati]

Indian Opinion, 21-3-1908

NOTES

1. *Vide* "My Experience in Gaol-II", 14-3-1908.
2. This has not been re-translated; for English text, *vide* "Petition to Director of Prisons", 21-1-1908. The last two sentences from it are, however, missing in the Gujarati translation.
3. Not available.

6
My Experience in Gaol–VI

PATIENTS

It would have been surprising if not one among 150 of us had been taken ill. The first casualty was Samunder Khan. He was ill even when he came to gaol and so was removed to hospital the day after his arrival. Mr. Karwa had an attack of rheumatism. for some the doctor treated him with ointment, etc., in the gaol. But later, he, too, was admitted to hospital. Two other prisoners fell sick and were removed to hospital. Since, it was hot and the prisoners were exposed to the sun outside some of them fell sick occasionally. They were treated as well as they could be [in goal]. Towards the end, Mr. Nawab Khan was also taken ill and, the day of his release, he had to be helped to walk. He improved after the doctor permitted him to drink milk. However, on the whole, the *Satyagrahi* prisoners kept well.

LACK OF SPACE

I mentioned earlier that our ward could accommodate 51 prisoners. The yard in front had the same capacity. When, towards the end, our number increased beyond 151, we experienced acute inconvenience. The Governor ordered tents to be pitched outside, and some of us were shifted to these. During the last few days, a hundred prisoners had to sleep outside. But they were brought back every morning, with the result that the yard turned out to be too small, and it was with great difficulty that room could be found for all the prisoners. On top of this, when we indulged in our vice of spitting were, there was danger of the place becoming dirty and infected.

Fortunately, people were amenable to persuasion and helped keep the yard clean. That how they managed to avoid illness. Anyone will admit that it was the Governments fault that so many prisoners were confined in so small a space. If the space was insufficient the Government ought not to have sent so many prisoners [to this gaol]. Had the movement continued, the Government would have found it impossible to accommodate any more.

READING

I mentioned earlier that the Governor had allowed us a table.[1] We were also given pens and an ink-pot. The gaol has a library which lends books to prisoners. I borrowed some of Carlyle's works and the *Bible*. From a Chinese interpreter who used to visit the place I borrowed a copy of the *Quran* in English, Huxley's lectures, Carlyle's biographies of Burns, Johnson and Scott, and Bacon's essays on civil and moral counsel. I also had some books of my own; these included an edition of the *Gita* with a commentary by Manilal Nabhubhai[2], some Tamil books, an Urdu book presented by Maulvi Saheb, the writings of Tolstoy, Ruskin and Socrates[3]. Most of these books I either read [for the first time] or re-read during my stay in gaol. I used to study Tamil regularly. In the morning I read the *Gita* and in the afternoon portions of the *Quran*. In the evening I used to explain the *Bible* to Mr. Fortoen, a Chinese Christian. As he wished to learn English, I taught it to him through the *Bible*. If I was going to serve my full term of two months in gaol, I had intended to complete the translation of one of Carlyle's books and another[4] of Ruskin. I believe these books would have kept me wholly occupied. If I had been awarded an even longer term, not only would I not have found it irksome, but I could have added usefully to my knowledge. I would have been quite contented. I believe that anyone who enjoys reading good books can easily bear to be alone anywhere.

Among my fellow-prisoners, Mr. C.M. Pillay, Mr. Naidoo and a few Chinese were in the habit of reading. Both the Naidoos had started learning Gujarati. During the last days a few books of Gujarati songs arrived, and many of us read these. But I do not call this reading.

DRILL

In gaol we cannot spend the whole day reading. Even if it were possible, we know that it is harmful in the long run. We therefore, managed, with some difficulty, to obtain the Governor's permission to learn the [P.T.] drill from the warder. A very kind man, he was only too happy to drill us morning and evening. It did us a lot of good too.

If we could have continued it sufficiently long, it would have done us all good. But the warder's work increased with the increase in the number of Indians, and the yard proved too small for the purpose.

The drill was, therefore, given up. However, we had Nawab Khan with us, and a drill of sorts was continued under his direction.

We also obtained the Governor's permission to work on the sewing machine. We tried to learn sewing pockets on to prisoners' [uniforms]. Mr. T. Naidoo and Mr. Easton, as they had an aptitude for the work, learnt it very quickly. It took me longer to pick it up. Before I had learnt it properly, there was a sudden increase in the number of prisoners and I had to leave off. The reader can thus see that given the will anyone can transform [even] a desert into a paradise. [Had our imprisonment continued,] we could have thus kept ourselves occupied with some work or the other, and no prisoner would have found his confinement irksome; on the contrary, he would have come out a better informed and abler man. There have been instances of conscientious men who achieved great things while in gaol. John Bunion bore up with prison life and wrote *The Pilgrim's Progress*, which proved an immortal work. The British rank it next to the *Bible*. Mr. Till wrote his *Orison* during his nine-month imprisonment in Bombay. Whether we are happy or miserable, whether we become good or bad in gaol or elsewhere depends entirely on our own mental attitudes.

VISITORS

Some Englishmen came to visit us in gaol. As a general rule, no prisoner is allowed visitors during the first month. Thereafter, each prisoner is allowed a visitor once a month, who must come on a Sunday[5]. The rule is relaxable in special circumstances. Mr. Phillips took advantage of this provision. The day after our arrival, he sought, and was granted, permission to visit Mr. Fortune, the Chinese Christian.

He also met the rest of us. He spoke a word of cheer to each of us, and then prayed, as was his wont. He managed to see us thrice.

Another clergyman, Rev. Advise, also took advantage of the same provision to visit us.

By special I permission Mr. Polak and Mr. Coven[6], too, came to see us once. He[7] was permitted to come only about [my] office work.

The warder is always present during a visit and all conversation must take place in his presence.

Mr. Cartwright, the editor of *The Transvaal Leader*, came thrice-by special permission each time. He came only with the object of bringing about a settlement. He was therefore, permitted to see us in private [that is, without the warder being present]. At his first meeting he formed an impression of what the Indian community would accept.

On the next occasion he brought with him the draft which he and other prominent Englishmen had prepared. After some alterations, it was signed by Mr. Quinn, Mr. Nadir and myself. This letter and the compromise having been dealt with at length elsewhere,[8] no more need be said about them here.

The Chief Magistrate, Mr. Playford, also visited us once. He was entitled to come at will. And it was not especially to see us that he came. But it is believed that he found time to come because we were all in gaol.

RELIGIOUS INSTRUCTION

It is now the practice in all western countries to provide religious instruction for prisoners. Accordingly, the Johannesburg Gaol has a chapel for Christians. But only white prisoners are allowed to worship there. I asked for special permission for myself and Mr. Fortoen, but I was told by the Governor that the church was open only to white Christians. They go to church every Sunday. They listen to sermons from clergymen of different denominations by turns. Some clergymen obtain special permission to preach to the Kaffirs too. They have, however, no chapel of their own. They therefore, sit in the gaol compound. The Jews have a rabbi to visit them.

But there is no corresponding arrangement for Hindus or Muslims. But then, there are not many Indian prisoners. All the same, it is rather humiliating that the religious needs of the Indian community should be ignored in gaol. Leaders of the two communities should give thought to this matter and arrange for instruction in both religions even if there should be only one Indian [in gaol]. The Maulvis and Hindu priests chosen for this work should be sincere men, otherwise their instruction is likely to be something of an infliction.

CONCLUSION

Much of what is worth knowing [about gaol life] has been discussed. It is necessary to give further thought to the fact of Indians being classed with Kaffirs in gaol. White prisoners are given a small bed each, a tooth-brush, and in addition to a towel, a handkerchief. We must ask to know why Indian prisoners also may not have these things.

One should not feel that these things are not worth bothering about. As the saying goes, drop by drop the lake fills. Similarly little things enhance or lower our prestige in the eyes of others. We read in the book Arab Wisdom that he who enjoys no respect has no religion.[9]

It is by defending their honour over a long period of time that nations achieve greatness. Honour does not mean arrogance; real honour consists in a state of mind that does not countenance the loss of a right, and in action flowing from such a state of mind. He alone can attain to such honour who really trusts—depends on—God. I am convinced that it is impossible for a man without sincere faith to discern the truth in every situation and act on it.

[From Gujarati] *Indian Opinion*, 28-3-1908.

NOTES

1. *Vide* "My Experience in Gaol[-II]", 14-3-1908.
2. Manilal Nabhubhai Dwivedi (1858-98); Sanskrit scholar, Gujarati poet, writer and journalist; author of several books on Indian philosophy; attended the Parliament of Religions along with Vivekananda.
3. Plato's Dialogues evidently, for it must have been about this time that Gandhiji started writing his Gujarati series, "Story of a Soldier of Truth".
4. *Unto This Last.*
5. It is not clear from the Gujarati whether a prisoner was allowed only one visitor a month or whether it was the visitor who might not meet more than one prisoner during a visit.
6. Ritch's father-in-law.
7. Polak.
8. *Vide* "Johannesburg Letter", 8-2-1908.
9. *Vide* also "Arab Wisdom", 28-12-1907.

Part Two

MY SECOND EXPERIENCE IN GAOL

7
My Second Experience in Gaol–I[1]

INTRODUCTION

I think my experience in gaol this time was better than in January 1908. It was good education for me personally, and I believe it will prove useful to other Indians.

A campaign of *Satyagraha* can take many forms, but it is found that gaol-going is the most effective means of fighting political disabilities. We shall have to go to gaol often enough, I think; it is necessary not only during the present agitation, but is the only course that can be adopted in fighting future disabilities. It is the duty of every Indian, therefore, to know all that is worth knowing about gaol-life.

ARRESTED

When Mr. Sorabji was arrested, I wished what I could follow him to gaol, or that the agitation would end before he was due to be released. I was disappointed. The same desire came over me again more intensely, when the brave leaders of Natal went to gaol, and [this time] it was fulfilled. While returning from Durban, I was arrested at Volksrust Station on October 7, 1908, for being without my certificate of voluntary registration and refusing to give my finger-impressions.

My object in going to Durban was to bring [along with me] educated Indians living in Natal and other Indians who had been previously resident in the Transvaal. I had hoped that quite a large number of Indians in Natal would show readiness to follow their leaders [to gaol]. The Government also felt the same way.

Accordingly, orders had been issued to the gaoler to make arrangements for the accommodation of more than a hundred Indians, and tents, blankets, utensils, etc., had been sent on from Pretoria. I also found, as I alighted at Volksrust accompanied by several Indians, that a large number of policemen were present. But all this labour proved superfluous. The gaoler and the police were disappointed, for only a small number of Indians from Natal had offered to accompany me. There were just six in that train. Eight more started from Durban by another train on the same day. In all, therefore, only fourteen Indians came. All of us were arrested and taken to the lock-up. The next day we were produced before the Magistrate, but the hearing of the case was postponed for seven days.

We declined to offer bail. Two days later, Mr Mavji Karsanji Kothari, who had joined [us] in spite of the fact that he was suffering from piles, was asked to bail himself out, as his trouble had become aggravated and there was need for a picket in Volksrust.

SITUATION IN GAOL

There were in gaol, when we arrived there, Mr. Dawad Mahomed, Mr. Rustomjee, Mr. Anglia and Mr. Sorabji Adajania who had initiated the second phase of the movement, and about 25 other Indians. It being the *Ramzan* month, Muslim friend had been observing the *roza*. By special permission, food was sent to them in the evening by Mr. Essop Suleman Kazi. Due to observance of the fast had thus been made possible. Though there is generally no provision for lighting in mofussil gaols, orders had been issued in view of the *Ramzan* to arrange for lights and provide a clock. Mr. Anglia led the *namaz*. Those who were observing the fast were subjected to hard labour during the first few days, but later on no hard labour was exacted from them.

As for the other Indians, permission had been granted for one of them to attend to the cooking. This was done by Mr. Umiyashanker Shelat and Mr. Surendrarai Medh, who were joined later by Mr. Joshi when the number of prisoners went up.

When these gentlemen were deported, cooking was attended to by Mr. Ratanshi Sodha, Mr. Raghavji and Mr. Mavji Kothari. Later still, when the number rose very high, Mr. Lalbhai and Mr. Omar Osman also joined. Those incharge of cooking had to get up at two or three in the morning and keep busy till five or six in the evening. When a considerable number of Indians had already been released, Mr. Moosa Essakji and Imam Saheb Bawazeer took charge of cooking. I count it as the good fortune of the Indians concerned that they were served food prepared by the Chairman of the Hamidia Islamic Society and a businessman who had in fact had no experience of cooking.

When the Imam Saheb and his companions were released, they left the legacy of cooking to me. Since I knew something of it, I experienced no difficulty. The work remained under my charge only for four days. It is now (that is, up to the moment of writing) being looked after by Mr. Harilal Gandhi. Though, the information as to who was incharge of cooking when we arrived in gaol does not fall under the heading [of this paragraph], I have given it here for the sake of convenience.

When we entered the gaol, Indians were lodged in three bedrooms. In this gaol, Indian and Kaffir prisoners were always lodged separately.

ARRANGEMENTS IN GAOLS

There are two wards in the prison for males; one for the whites and one for the Kaffirs—the gaol [also] accommodates other non-whites.

Though they were free thus to lodge the Indians in the Kaffir ward, the gaoler had made provision for them in the ward for the whites.

There are small cells, each with arrangements to accommodate ten or fifteen or even more prisoners. The prison is built entirely of stone. The cell has a good height. The walls are plastered and the floor is washed so that it always stays very clean. Moreover, the walls are frequently whitewashed, so that they always appear fresh. The area in front is paved with black stone, and is washed every day. It has a water-spout which enables three men to bathe simultaneously. There are two lavatories, and also benches. Above, there is a barbedwire covering intended to prevent prisoners from escaping by climbing the walls. Every room is well-lighted and properly ventilated. The prisoners are locked in at six in the evening, and let out at six in the morning. The cell is locked from outside during the night. This means that, if anyone has a call of nature to answer, he cannot go out of the cell, and hence commodes, filled with water treated with a germicide, are placed in the cell itself.

DIET

At the time of my imprisonment in Volksrust, the Indian prisoners were served mealie pap in the morning, and rice, with some vegetable, for the mid-day and evening meals. The vegetable served was mostly potato. No ghee was allowed at all. Under-trial prisoners were allowed, in addition, an ounce of sugar with mealie pap in the morning, and half a pound of bread for the mid-day meal. Some of the under-trial prisoners used to share a portion of their bread and sugar with the prisoners undergoing sentences after conviction.

Prisoners were entitled to meat twice (a week); since, however, it was not given to either the Hindus or the Muslims, they were entitled to a substitute. We, therefore, made a joint petition[2] and as a result it was ordered that we should receive an ounce of ghee and, on meat days, half a pound of beans in place of meat. Moreover, there was some *tandalja* growing by itself in the gaol garden, and we were allowed to pluck its leaves. We were also permitted from time to time to gather onions from the garden. There remained, therefore, nothing to complain of about food after ghee and beans had been sanctioned.

The diet in the Johannesburg Gaol is somewhat different. There, only ghee is supplied with rice; no vegetables are allowed. In the evenings, there are green vegetables and mealie pap twice in the week, beans on three days, and potatoes, with mealie pap, once.

Though this scale cannot be considered adequate, as judged by our habits, it is not bad in itself. Many Indians have a strong dislike of mealie pap and obstinately refuse to have it. But personally I think this is an error. Mealie pap is a sweet and strength-giving food. It can be taken in place of wheat in this country. It is very tasty when sugar is added to it, but even otherwise it tastes quite good when one is hungry. If one can get used to it, the foregoing scale will not prove inadequate nourishment; on the contrary, one may actually thrive on it. With some adjustments, it can be a perfect diet. But it is a matter of regret that we have grown so fond of good eating and have pampered ourselves into such habits that we are quick to lose our temper if we do not get the food we are used to. This was my experience in Volksrust, and it made me very unhappy. There was incessant grumbling about food, and very often there were such fretful scenes as if eating and living were the same thing, or as if we lived only to eat. Surely it does not become a *Satyagrahi* to behave in this manner.

It is our duty to try to get some changes made in the diet. If we fail, however, we must remain content with whatever is offered and thus demonstrate to the Government our determination not to yield; this also is our duty. There are some Indians who are afraid of going to gaol only because of the inconvenience in the matter of food. They must make a conscious effort to overcome the craving for good food that might have enslaved them.

SENTENCED TO IMPRISONMENT

As I mentioned above, all our cases were postponed for seven days, so that they came up for hearing on the 14th, when some of us were sentenced to a month and others to six weeks with hard labour.

There was a boy eleven years old who was sentenced to 14 days' simple imprisonment. I was much worried lest the case against me should be withdrawn. The Magistrate retired for some time after the other cases had been disposed off, which made me all the more nervous. The view generally expressed earlier was that I would be charged with failure to produce my register and refusal to give my thumb-impression, and also with inciting other Indians to enter the Transvaal without any right. While I was grappling with the problem in my mind, the Magistrate returned to the court and my case was called out. I was then sentenced to a fine of Rs. 25 or to two months' hard labour. This made me very happy, and I congratulated myself on what I considered to be my good fortune in being allowed to join the others in gaol.

CLOTHES

After the sentence was passed, we were issued gaol uniforms. We were supplied each with a pair of short breeches, a shirt of coarse cloth, a jumper, a cap, a towel and a pair of socks and sandals. I think this is a very convenient dress for work. It is simple, and wears well.

We should have nothing to complain about such a dress. We should not mind having it even for everyday wear. The dress given to the whites is somewhat different. They get a rimmed cap, stockings and handkerchief, in addition to two towels. Indians, too, need to be supplied with handkerchiefs.

(To be continued)

[From Gujarati]

Indian Opinion, 2-1-1909

NOTES

1. For articles on his first experience, *vide* Vol. VIII.
2. *Vide* "Petition to Resident Magistrate", 11-10-1908.

8
My Second Experience in Gaol–II

WORK

The Government can exact nine hours' labour daily from those sentenced to rigorous imprisonment. The prisoners are locked in every day at six O'clock. At half-past five in the morning, there is a bell to wake them up, and the cell-doors open at six. The prisoners are counted when they are locked in and again when they are let out. In order that the counting may be orderly and speedy, every prisoner is required to stand at attention near his bed. Each one must roll up his bedding, put it in its proper place and, after a wash, be ready before six. Then, at seven, work starts. The work assigned is of various kinds.

On the first day, we had to dig up the soil in a field near the main road for purposes of cultivation.[1] About 30 Indians were there. No one was thus compelled to work if he was not fit enough. We were taken there along with the Kaffirs. The soil was very hard, and since it had to be dug up with spades, the labour involved was strenuous. The day was very hot. The place of work must have been at a distance of about one and a half miles from the gaol. All the Indians set to work with great energy. But only a few of them were used to hard work, so that we were all quite exhausted with the exertion. Among us was Ravikrishna, son of Babu Talevantsingh. I was much disconcerted to see him work, and yet the energy with which he went about it gladdened my heart. As the day advanced, we found the task quite hard. The warder was rather sharp of temper. He shouted at the prisoners all the time to keep on working. The more he shouted, the more nervous the Indians became. I even saw some of them in tears. One, I noticed, had a swollen foot. I was sorely distressed at this.

However, I went on urging everyone to ignore the warder and carry on as best he could. I too got exhausted. There were large blisters on the palms, the lymph oozing out of them. It was difficult to bend down, and the spade seemed to weight a maund. For myself, I was praying to God all the time to save my honour, so that I might not break down, and to give me strength to keep doing the work as well as I should. Placing my trust in Him, I went on with the work. The warder started rebuking me. He did so because I was resting. I told him that there was no need to shout at me, that I would do my best and work to the utmost limit of endurance. Just then, I observed Mr. Jhinabhai Desai fainting away. I paused a little, not being allowed to leave the place of work. The warder went to the spot. I found that I, too, must go, and I ran. Two other Indians also followed me. Water was sprinkled over Jhinabhai. He came to. The warder sent away the others to their work. I was allowed to remain by his side. After plenty of cold water had been poured over Jhinabhai's head, he felt somewhat better. I told the warder that Jhinabhai would not be able to walk down to the gaol. Hence, a cab was sent for. I was ordered to take him in it to the gaol. As I splashed cold water over Jhinabhai's head, I thought to myself, "A great many Indians have been going to gaol at my word. What a sinner I would be if I had been giving wrong advice ! Am I the cause of all this suffering on the part of Indians?" As I thought thus, I sighed deeply. I considered the matter afresh, with God as witness, and, after being plunged in reflection for some time, I collected myself with a smile. I felt I had given the right advice. If to bear suffering is in itself a kind of happiness, there is no need to be worried by it. This was only a case of fainting but even if it were to be death, I could have given no other advice. Seeing that our sole duty was to break free from our fetters by enduring every hardship rather than remaining bound for life, I felt light in heart and tried to instil courage in Jhinabhai.

As soon as the cab arrived, Jhinabhai was made to lie down in it and was taken away. A complaint was made to the chief warder. After inquiry, the warder was reprimanded. Jhinabhai was not taken out for work at noon. Similarly, four other Indians were found too weak [to work]. All the others resumed work. One is required to work from twelve noon to one. At noon, supervision over us was assigned to a Kaffir warder instead of a white one. He proved a little better. He did not go on prodding us. Occasionally, he would shout a few words.

Moreover, at noon Kaffirs and Indians were deployed in the same place, though at different spots. We were given softer soil to dig up.

I had a talk with the contractor. He said that the labour of Indian prisoners was likely to put him to some loss. He admitted that Indians could not all at once equal the Kaffirs in point of physical strength. I also told him that they were not likely to work [harder] for fear of the warder, that they would do as much—and only as much—as they possibly could for fear of God. But I found it necessary later to revise this idea altogether. Let us see how that happened.

We were taken out [again] the next day. But we were sent with a Kaffir warder instead of a white one. The Kaffir, moreover, was not the same one as on the previous day. He had been advised not to bother us at all about work.

(To be continued)
[From Gujarati]

Indian Opinion, 9-1-1909

NOTES

1. Later, this became the subject of a controversy; *vide* Appendix VII.

9
My Second Experience in Gaol–III

We were advised to make a sincere attempt to do our best. The work assigned to us was also light. We had to dig up pits and fill them on municipal land adjoining the main road. This allowed occasional rest. But I found from experience that, left to our conscience and our God, we are shirkers. For I observed that the men slackened in their work.

It is my confirmed belief that we get a bad name because of this habit of shirking work and also that this habit is one of the reasons why our struggle is being prolonged. *Satyagraha* is a difficult as well as an easy method, our *bona fides* must not be in doubt. We bear no ill will to the Government. We do not regard it as our enemy. If we are fighting it, it is with a view to correcting its errors and making it mend its ways. We would not be happy to see it in difficulties. We believe that even our resistance is for its good. It follows from this line of reasoning that we at any rate should work to the best of our ability in gaol. If we believe that we have no moral obligation to work [hard], it is not right that we put in the full amount of work in the presence of the warder. If it is not just that we should work, then we should not submit to the warder, but resist him rather and suffer any further term of imprisonment that may be awarded to us in consequence. But there is no Indian who holds such a view. If some of them do not work [hard enough], there is no more to it than mere laziness and desire to shirk work. It does not become us thus to be lazy or to shirk work. As *Satyagrahis*, it is our duty to do whatever work is given to us; if we worked [as well as we could] without any fear of the warder, we would be spared all harassment. There would then be no question of our being made to overwork ourselves. Because of the habit of shirking work, people were put to some difficulties in gaol.

After this digression, let us return to the main story. As days passed, our work became lighter, as I have pointed out above. The batch which included me was next assigned the task of maintaining cleanliness in the gaol garden and looking after its cultivation. Our work was mainly to sow maize seeds, clear the potato bed and dust the potato plants.

And then, for two days, they took us to dig a municipal tank. Our work there consisted of digging, piling up the earth and carrying it away in barrows. This again was hard work. We had a taste of it only for two days. I had a swollen wrist, which was cured when treated with earth.

The place being at a distance of four or five miles, we used to be taken there in a trolley. We had to cook our meal near the tank, so that we also carried with us the necessary provisions and fuel. Here, too, the contractor was not satisfied. We could not equal to the Kaffirs. After making us work on the tank for two days, they gave us some other work. Hitherto they used to take out mostly such Indians as were strong enough for work. Now, however, they were formed into groups. Some of them were sent to dig out the weeds that had shot up round the soldiers' tombs. Others were sent to clean the graveyard.

This arrangement continued for some time. Meanwhile, after the Barberton case, nearly 50 Indians were released.

During the remaining period, we were assigned work in the garden. This included digging, reaping, sweeping, etc. This cannot be considered to be heavy work; rather, it was conductive to vigour of health. One may at first get bored when engaged on such work for nine hours at a stretch, but one doesn't feel it after getting used to it.

Apart from the kind of work described above, it is the duty of the men in every cell to carry the bucket for urine, etc., placed in it. I observed that our people are unwilling to do such work. In fact, there is no reason why one should mind it. It is wrong to think of any work as humiliating or degrading. Moreover, those who have offered themselves for imprisonment cannot afford to stand on prestige thus. I saw that sometimes there was some argument as to who should carry the urine bucket. If we have understood the full meaning of *Satyagraha*, we would compete with one another in offering to do such work, instead of making difficulties about it, and one would feel honoured if the work fell to one's lot. That is to say, the honour would not consist in being required by the Government to work, but, since the work had in any case to be attended to, he who was the first to offer himself would deserve special honour.

Since, we have resolved to bear all suffering, each one of us may as well come forward to suffer more than others, and he who suffers most should feel most honoured. An example of this was once set by Mr. Hassan Mirza. He has been suffering from a very bad disease of the lungs. He is delicate of health. All the same, he gladly took upon himself whatever work fell to his lot from day-to-day. Furthermore, he gave no thought to his health. Once, Kaffir warder asked him to clean the chief warder's privy, which he instantly started doing. As he had never done such work, he vomited. He was not upset by this, while he was cleaning another privy, I happened to come up and see him engaged upon the work. I was astonished. To be sure, I felt great affection for him. On inquiry, I learnt about the first privy. Another time, the same Kaffir warder was ordered by the chief [warder] to find two Indians to clean the latrines specially set apart for the Indians. The warder approached me about this and asked me to name two persons.

I thought I was the best person for such work, and so I went myself. Personally, I feel no shame in this kind of work. I think we should accustom ourselves to it. Because of the dislike we feel for such work, not only do we find the front of our houses and our lavatories generally dirty, but also originate, or spread, epidemics such as the plague, etc. We assume that lavatories are bound to be unclean, and thus we frequently invite the charge of being dirty. Once an Indian was sentenced to solitary confinement, that is to say, he was locked up in a cell by himself, for refusing to do such work. Of course, I see nothing wrong in our having to submit to any kind of sentence. But, in this particular case, the penalty could have been avoided. It is, moreover, not proper that we should hold ourselves back from such work. When I set out to attend to the work, the warder began to scold others and urged them to come forward. This spread the news about the order and forthwith Mr. Omar Osman and Mr. Rustomjee ran to my help; the work was very light, though. My object in narrating this story is to show that these men also felt honoured in doing such work when required by the Government. If we are hurt by the nature of the work assigned to us, we cannot take part in any fight worth the name.

REMOVED TO JOHANNESBURG

I have given above an account of the work (assigned to us) in Volksrust Gaol. But I did not spend two full months in that gaol. I was suddenly sent away to Johannesburg for a few days. What happened there is worth recounting. I was taken there on October 25.

The reason was that I was required to give evidence in the case of Dahya, the tailor. There were all kinds of speculations as to other possible reasons. Everyone was filled with hope and imagined that perhaps there might be an interview with General Smuts. It was found later that there was no such idea. A warder was specially sent from Johannesburg to fetch me. A railway compartment was placed at our disposal. We had second-class tickets, the only reason being that there were no third-class carriages in the train. It appears that prisoners are carried only in third-class compartments. I was in gaol uniform throughout the journey. I had some luggage with me, which I was made to carry myself. The distance from the gaol to the station had to be covered on foot. After arriving at Johannesburg, I had (again) to reach the gaol on foot, carrying the luggage myself. The incident provoked strong comments in newspapers. Questions were asked in the British Parliament. Many persons felt hurt. Everyone thought that, being a political prisoner, I should not have been made to walk the distance, dressed in gaol uniform and carrying a load.[1]

One can understand why this should have given offence to some people. When Mr. Anglia came to know how I was to go, there were tears in his eyes. Mr. Naidoo and Mr. Polak were at the station to see me, having received information (about my arrival). They were also touched to see my condition. There is no reason why one should feel these things so much. It is not likely that in this country the Government will make any distinction between political and other prisoners. The greater the harassment we suffer, the earlier shall we win our release. Moreover, we shall find on reflection that it is not much of a hardship to have to wear a gaol uniform, or go on foot or carry one's luggage. But the world will always think of these things as hardships and that is why an outcry was raised in England.

I did not have the slightest trouble from the warder during the journey. I had resolved (while in Volksrust Gaol) that, unless openly allowed by the warder, I would not take any food other than what I was allowed in gaol. Hence, I had carried on with the gaol diet all these days. But they had given me no food packet for the journey. The warder (accompanying me) allowed me to buy whatever food I wanted. The station master offered me some money. He was also very much upset [to observe my condition]. I thanked him, [but] declined his offer of money. I borrowed 10s from Mr. Kazi, who was present at the station, and spent something from it to buy food for myself and for the warder on the train.

It was evening when we reached Johannesburg, so that I was not taken where I could be among other Indians. I was given a bed in a cell of the prison where there were mostly Kaffir prisoners who had been lying ill. I spent the night in his cell in grest misery and fear. I did not know that the very next day I would be taken among our own people, and, thinking that I would be kept in this place all the time, I became quite nervous. I felt extremely uneasy, but I resolved in my mind that my duty required me to bear every suffering. I read the *Bhagavad Gita* which I had carried with me. I read the verses which had a bearing on my situation and, meditating on them, managed to compose myself.

The reason why I felt so uneasy was that the Kaffir and Chinese prisoners appeared to be wild, murderous and given to immoral ways. I did not know their language. A Kaffir started putting question to me. I felt a hint of mockery even in this. I did not understand what it was. I returned no reply. He asked me in broken English why I had been brought there in that fashion. I gave a brief reply, and then I lapsed into silence. Then came a Chinese. He appeared to be worse.

He came near the bed and looked closely at me. I kept still. Then he went to a Kaffir lying in bed. The two exchanged obscene jokes, uncovering each other's genitals. Both these prisoners had charges of murder and larceny against them. Knowing this, how could I possibly sleep? Thinking that I would bring this to the notice of the Governor the next day, I fell asleep for a while late in the night.

Real suffering lies in this. Carrying luggage and such other troubles are nothing very serious. Realizing that the experience I have had must also sometimes be that of other Indians, and that they too would feel the fear that I did, I was happy that I had suffered in the same way as others. The experience, I thought, would impel me to agitate against the Government all the more tenaciously, and I hoped that I might succeed in inducing prison reforms in regard to these matters. All these are indirect benefits of *Satyagraha*.

As soon as we rose the following day, I was taken to where the other prisoners were lodged, so that I had no chance to complain to the Governor about what had happened. I have, though, resolved in my mind on an agitation to ensure that Indian prisoners are not lodged with Kaffirs or others. When I arrived at the place, there were about 15 Indian prisoners. Except for three, all of them were *Satyagrahis*. The three were charged with other offences. These prisoners were generally lodged with Kaffirs. When I reached there, the chief warder issued an order that all of us should be lodged in a separate room. I observed with regret that some Indians were happy to sleep in the same room as the Kaffirs, the reason being that they hoped there for a secret supply of tobacco, etc. This is a matter of shame to us. We may entertain no aversion to Kaffirs, but we cannot ignore the fact that there is no common ground between them and us in the daily affairs of life. Moreover, those who wish to sleep in the same room with them have ulterior motives for doing so. Obviously, we ought to abandon such notions if we want to make progress.

(To be continued)
[From Gujarati]

Indian Opinion, 16-1-1909

NOTE

1. *Vide* Treatment in prison: (a) marched in concict's farb, 31-10-1908.

10
My Second Experience in Gaol–IV

I had one further unpleasant experience in the Johannesburg Gaol. In this gaol, there are two different kinds of wards. One ward is for Kaffir and Indian prisoners sentenced to hard labour. The other is for prisoners who are called as witnesses and those who have been sentenced to imprisonment in civil proceedings. Prisoners sentenced to hard labour have no right to go into this second ward. We slept in it, but we could not use its lavatory as of right. In the first ward, the number of prisoners wanting the use of the lavatory is so large that a visit to it is a great nuisance. Some Indians find this a source of great inconvenience. I was one of them. I was told by the warder that there would be no harm in my using a lavatory in the second ward. I, therefore, went to one of the lavatories in this ward. At these lavatories, too, there is usually a crowd. Moreover, the lavatories have open access. There are no doors. As soon as I had occupied one of them, there came along a strong, heavily-built, fearful-looking Kaffir. He asked me to get out and started abusing me. I said I would leave very soon. Instantly he lifted me up in his arms and threw me out.

Fortunately, I caught hold of the door-frame, and saved myself from a fall. I was not in the least frightened by this. I smiled and walked away; but one or two Indian prisoners who saw what had happened started weeping. Since, they could not offer any help in gaol, they felt helpless and miserable. I heard later that other Indians also had to go through similar tribulations. I acquainted the Governor with what had happened and told him there was urgent need for separate lavatories for Indians.

I also told him that Indian prisoners should never be lodged with Kaffirs. The Governor immediately issued an order for a lavatory for Indians to be sent on from the Central Gaol. Thus, from the next day the difficulty about lavatories disappeared.[1] As for myself, I had no motions for four days, and hence I suffered in health somewhat.

While in Johannesburg, I was taken to the court three or four times. I was allowed to see Mr. Polak and my son there. Others also came sometimes. I was even free, when in the court, to have food brought to me from home and accordingly Mr. Kallenbach used to bring bread, cheese, etc., for me.

When I was in this gaol, the number of *Satyagrahi* prisoners in it mounted very high. At one time, there were more than 50. Many of them were asked to pound gravel with a small hammer, sitting on a stone. About 10 men were employed in mending torn clothes. I was given the work of stitching caps with a sewing machine. I learnt sewing for the first time here. It was not difficult work and therefore I learnt it in no time.

Most of the Indians were employed in pounding gravel. I also asked for the same work. But the warder said that he had orders from the chief warder not to let me out, and accordingly he did not allow me to go out for pounding gravel. One day it so happened that I had no sewing work to do on the machine or other work. I, therefore, started to read. The rule is that every prisoner must do some work or other assigned to him in the gaol. The warder therefore, called me and inquired whether I was ill.

I replied: No.

Q. Why are you then not doing any work?

A. I have finished the work assigned to me. I do not wish merely to pretend being busy with work. If you give me any work, I shall be glad to do it. Otherwise, what harm is there if I read, having nothing else to do?

Q. That is true, but it will be better if you remain in the store when the chief warder or the Governor comes round.

A. I don't like to do so. I am going to tell the Governor also that there isn't sufficient work in the store and that I should therefore, be taken out to pound gravel.

Q. All right. I cannot on my own send you out for that.

A little later, the Governor came. I told him everything. He did not allow me to go out for pounding gravel, but informed me that it was not necessary either, since I was to be sent back to Volksrust the following day.

MEDICAL EXAMINATION—UNDRESSING OF PRISONERS

The freedom from some regulations which is permitted in the mofussil Gaol of Volksrust is not possible in the Central Gaol of Johannesburg. For instance, in Volksrust Mr. Dawad Mahomed was allowed to have a shawl as head-dress, and breeches were allowed to others as well. Mr. Rustomjee, Mr. Sorabji and Mr. Shapurji were permitted to wear their own caps. This will not be easy in the Johannesburg Gaol. Similarly, when prisoners first come to gaol, they are examined by the physician. This is done in order to find out if any of them suffers from a contagious disease and, if anyone does, to give him treatment and isolate him from the others. For this reason, the prisoners are examined with great care. Some of the prisoners are found to suffer from diseases like syphilis, and therefore, everyone of them has his genitals examined. For this purpose, the prisoners are totally undressed, while being examined. Unlike the others, Kaffirs are kept standing undressed for nearly 15 minutes so as to save the physician's time. Indian prisoners are made to lower their breeches only when the physician approaches them. The other garments have to be removed in advance. Almost every Indian resents having to lower his breeches, but most of them do not create any difficulty in the interest of our movement, though at heart they feel ill at ease. I told the physician about this. As a special case, he examined some of the prisoners in the store but declined to adopt that as a practice. The Association has written about this,[2] and the matter is under correspondence. We are justified in making an issue of this. This is an old practice of these people,[3] which is not likely to be changed all at once. All the same, the matter deserves attention.

When in the presence of men only, there should be on need to conceal any parts of our anatomy. There is no reason to believe, moreover, that others will keep staring at the parts which we generally hide. We need not have any false sense of shame. If we are pure in our own minds, where is the need to be particular about hiding what is a part of our natural endowment? I know that these ideas will sound strange to every Indian, but I do feel that one must go deep into the matter and learn the right attitude to take. By raising difficulties of this nature, we harm our cause in the long run. Formerly, Indian prisoners were not examined by the physician at all. But once two or three Indians were interrogated. They replied that they had no disease.

The physician examined them nevertheless, having felt somewhat suspicious, and found that they had not spoken the truth. He decided thenceforth to examine even Indian prisoners. We can thus see that whenever we are in some trouble, it is generally of our own making.

RETURN FROM JOHANNESBURG

As I said above, I was taken back to Volksrust Gaol on November 4.

This time, too, I was accompanied by a warder. I was dressed in the prisoner's uniform, but on this occasion, instead of being made to walk, I was taken in a cab. However, instead of second, third-class tickets were provided. By way of provisions for the journey, I was given half a pound of bread and bully-beef. I refused the latter, giving up my claim to it. On the way, I was permitted by the warder to buy some other food. When I reached the station, I found some Indian tailors present. They noticed me. Of course, talking was not allowed.

Observing my dress, etc., some of them were filled with tears. Since, I was not free even to tell them that I did not mind my dress or anything else, I merely remained a silent spectator. The two of us were assigned a separate compartment. There was a tailor travelling in the adjoining compartment, who passed on some of his food to me. At Heidelberg, Mr. Somabhai met me. He bought for me some eatables on the station. The woman from whom he bought them at first refused to accept any money, showing her sympathy for our cause. When Mr. Somabhai insisted on paying, she merely accepted a nominal sum of six pence. Since, Mr. Somabhai had also sent a telegram to Standerton, several Indians had gone to the station there too, carrying some food with them. The warder and I had therefore, more than our fill on the way.

As soon as we reached Volksrust, I was met by Mr. Nagadi and Mr. Kazi at the station. Both of them walked with me part of the way.

They were permitted to walk at some distance from us. I was again made to walk the distance from the station [to the gaol], and carry my luggage. The matter even provoked much comment in newspapers.

All the Indians were happy to find me back in Volksrust. I was locked up in Mr. Dawad Mahomed's cell for the night, so that we kept awake till a late hour narrating our experiences to each other.

SITUATION OF INDIAN PRISONERS

When I returned to Volksrust, the situation of Indian prisoners had assumed a new aspect altogether. The number of prisoners had risen from about 30 to about 75. There was no way of accommodating such numbers in that gaol. Eight tents had therefore been pitched. For cooking, a special *chulha* had been sent from Pretoria. Moreover, the prisoners were often allowed to go to a river nearby for a bath. The men looked like soldiers rather than prisoners.

This was not a prison, but a camp of *Satyagrahis*. What, then, did it matter whether we were treated well or ill by the warders? In fact, most of the warders were on the whole reasonable men. Mr. Dawad Mahomed had given a nick-name to every warder. One was called "Oakly", another "Mafuto", and so on.

VISITORS

We used to get a good number of Indian visitors in Volksrust Gaol. Mr. Kazi was always hanging around. He looked after the prisoners' affairs outside, putting his whole heart into the work, and seized every opportunity to visit us. Mr. Polak used to come almost every week on official work. Mr. Mahomed Ibrahim and Mr. Kharsani came specially from Natal in connection with contributions to the Congress funds by Main Line Indians. On

Id day, about a hundred Indian businessmen from Natal must have paid us a visit.

There was also a shower of telegrams on that day.

SOME OBSERVATIONS

Prisons are generally kept very clean. If this were not so, there would be epidemics before long. But there is also lack of cleanliness in some respects. Blankets are constantly interchanged. A blanket that has been used by the dirtiest of Kaffirs may later fall to an Indian's lot. Frequently, the blankets are found to be full of lice. They have a nasty smell. Under the rules, they must be exposed to sunlight for half an hour every day, if the sky is clear. But this is rarely done. The difficulty about blankets is not a trivial matter to a man of clean habits.

The same thing often happens about dress. The uniform worn by a prisoner is not always washed after he is released, but is given to another prisoner to wear in the same dirty condition. This is a disturbing state of affairs.

Moreover, there was considerable crowding of prisoners. In Johannesburg, where the accommodation was just sufficient for 200 prisoners, nearly 400 were lodged. Thus, twice the number of prisoners permitted under the rules was often lodged in a cell, and sometimes there were not enough blankets to go round. This was not an inconsiderable difficulty. But it is a law of nature that man adjusts himself to any situation in which he is placed by circumstances beyond his control. This happened with the Indian prisoners too.

Even in the midst of the very real difficulties mentioned above, Mr. Dawad Mahomed, especially, remained in good spirits the whole day and kept the Indian prisoners amused all the time by his wit and humour.

There was an incident in the Gaol which made one unhappy.

Once a Kaffir warder approached some Indians who were sitting in a group. He asked for two Indians to go with him and do some grassmowing. No one spoke for some time. Mr. Imam Abdool Kadir then offered himself for the work. Even then, no one got ready to accompany him. On the contrary, they told the warder that Mr. Kadir was their priest and asked him not to set him any task. This made matters twice as bad. For one thing, everyone ought to have offered himself for the work, instead of which, when the Imam Saheb came forward, out of consideration for the good name of the community, they divulged his status. By indicating their unwillingness to take up the work even when the Imam Saheb was ready for it, they proved that we–the community as a whole–are a shameless lot.

(To be continued)
[From Gujarati]

Indian Opinion, 23-1-1909

NOTES

1. The incident was later discussed in the Press; *vide* Appendix X.
2. In two letters, dated November 24 and December 1, 1908, the British Indian Association protested to the Governor of the Transvaal Gaol against the practice of keeping prisoners undressed for over an hour in public for medical examination. The Director of Prisons, replying to these representations, denied that the prisoners were kept in such condition longer than necessary for the check-up. This correspondence was published in *Indian Opinion*, 19-12-1908. The Transvaal Ministers, also, in a minute dated January 30, 1909 refuted the allegation.
3. This might also have been intended to mean: the prejudice against undressing in public is an old sentiment of our people which cannot be given up all at once.

11
My Second Experience in Gaol–V

MORAL DILEMMA

When I had completed about half the term of my imprisonment, there was a telegram from Phoenix saying that Mrs. Gandhi was seriously ill and asking me to go down immediately.[1] Everyone was unhappy at this. I had no doubt as to my duty. When the gaoler asked me whether I would agree to pay the fine to obtain my release, I replied without the slightest hesitation that I would never do so, and that it was implied in our movement that we should bear separation from out kith and kin. The gaoler smiled at this, but felt sorry too. On a superficial view of the matter, this attitude would appear to be rather harsh, but personally I am convinced that that is the only right attitude to adopt. I think of my love for the motherland as an aspect of my religion. It is, of course, not the whole of religion. But religion cannot be considered to be complete without it. If necessary, we should bear separation from our family in order to be able to follow the dictates of our religion. We may even have to lose them. Not only is there no cruelty in this, but it is actually our duty to do so. If it is true that we have pledged ourselves to fight unto death, there is nothing further to think of. Lord Roberts lost his only son for a cause inferior to ours and, being on the front, could not even attend his funeral. This history of the world is full of such instances.

QUARRELS AMONG KAFFIRS

There are some dangerous murderers among the Kaffir prisoners in gaol. We find these prisoners constantly engaged in disputes. After they are locked up in the cell, they quarrel among themselves. Sometimes, they openly defy the warder. One warder was twice assaulted by the prisoners. Indian prisoners are obviously in danger when locked up in the same cell with these. So far, Indians have not been placed in such a situation. But so long as Indian prisoners are classed with the Kaffirs, the danger will remain.

ILLNESS IN GAOL

There was for the most part no serious illness among the prisoners. I have already mentioned Mr. Mavji's case. There was a Tamil named Mr. Raju, who had acute dysentery. He was very much pulled down. The reason he gave for this was that he used to take 30 cups of tea every day, and he got dysentery because he did not get them. He asked for tea. Of course, the request was rejected. But he was given some medicine, and the medical officer in the Gaol ordered two pounds of milk and bread [for him]. This restored him to full health.

Mr. Ravikrishna Talevantsingh kept indifferent health till the end. Mr. Kazi and Mr. Bawazeer were ill all the time. Mr. Ratanshi Sodha was observing a religious vow for the four months of the rainy season, and therefore he had only one meal a day. Since, the food was not quite satisfactory, he nearly starved himself and as a result got oedema. A part from these, there were other cases of minor illness.

On the whole, however, we found that even those Indians who fell ill were not broken in spirit. They were happy to bear this particular kind of hardship for the sake of the motherland.

SOME DIFFICULTIES

It was observed that the more irritating difficulties were those of our own making rather than those created by others. There were occasions in the gaol when one sensed in the air distinctions between Hindus and Muslims, between high and low castes. Indians of all communities and castes lived together in the Gaol, which gave one an opportunity to observe how backward we are in the matter of self-government.

It was also discovered, however, that we were not altogether incapable of self-government, for whatever difficulties cropped up were always overcome in the end.

Some Hindus said that they were not prepared to take food prepared by Muslims or by certain individuals. Men who hold such views should never stir out of India. I also observed that no objection was raised if any Kaffir or white touched our food. It so happened once that someone objected to sleeping near a certain person on the ground that the latter belonged to the scavenger caste. This again was humiliating to us. On probing deeper into the matter, it was found that the objection was raised not because the man [who had raised the objection] was himself particular about it, but because he was afraid of being declared an outcaste should other members of his community in India come to hear of it. Thanks to these hypocritical distinctions of high and low and to the fear of subsequent caste tyranny, we have, I think, turned our back on truth and embraced falsehood. How can we be called *Satyagrahis* if, knowing that it is wrong to despise the scavenger, we still do so out of an unreasonable fear of members of our caste or other men? I wish that Indians who join this movement also resort to *Satyagraha* against their caste and their family and against evil wherever they find it. As for myself, I am convinced that it is because we do not act in this way that the successful outcome of our struggle is being delayed. If it is true that we are all Indians, how can we cling to false distinctions and so quarrel among ourselves and, at the same time, demand our rights? How can we hope to achieve success in our struggle if, out of fear of what may happen to us in India, we do not do what we believe to be right? It is the mark of a coward to shrink from anything out of mere fear, and Indians who are cowards will not hold out to the last in this great war that is being waged against the Government.

WHO CAN GO TO GAOL?

We see from these facts that those who are slaves to bad habits, who observe vain distinctions of caste and community, who are quarrel-some, who are not able to look on Hindus and Muslims with an equal eye and those who are diseased in body—such men cannot go to Gaol or remain in gaol for any length of time.

It follows therefore, that those who want to go to gaol as a matter of honour and with a view to the welfare of the motherland must be healthy in body, mind and soul. An ailing man will find himself exhausted in the end; those who are conscious of Hindu-Muslim differences, who think themselves superior to others, who are slaves to bed habits, who are possessed by a craving for tea, smoking or such other things, are incapable of fighting till the bitter end.

WHAT I READ IN GAOL

Though the entire day is taken up with work, one can find time for some reading in the mornings and evenings, as also on Sundays and, since there is nothing else to tax one's attention in gaol, it is possible to read with a peaceful mind. Though I had limited time on my hand, I managed to read two books by the great Ruskin, the essays of the great Thoreau, some portions of the *Bible*, life of Garibaldi (in Gujarati), essays of Lord Bacon (in Gujarati), and two other books about India. We can find the doctrine of *Satyagraha* in the writings of Ruskin and Thoreau. The Gujarati books were sent by Mr. Diwan for all of us to read. Apart from these works, I read the *Bhagavad Gita* almost every day. All this reading had the effect of confirming my belief in *Satyagraha*, and I can say today that life in gaol is not in the least boring.

TWO ATTITUDES

We can take two different attitudes to what I have written above.

First, why should we bear such hardships, submit ourselves, for instance, to the restrictions of gaol life, wear coarse and ungainly dress, eat food which is hardly food, starve ourselves, suffer being kicked by the warder, live among the Kaffirs, do every kind of work, whether we like it or not, obey a warder who is only good enough to be our servant, be unable to receive any friends or write letters, go without things that we may need, and sleep in company with robbers and thieves? Better die than suffer this. Better pay the fine than go to gaol. Let no one be punished with gaol. Such an attitude will make a man quite weak and afraid of imprisonment, and he will achieve nothing good by being in gaol.

Alternatively, one may consider oneself fortunate to be in gaol in the cause of the motherland, in defence of one's honour and one's religion. Gaol life, one may think, involves no [real] suffering. Outside, one has to carry out the will of many, whereas one has only the warder to reckon with in Gaol. One has no anxieties in gaol, no problem of earning one's livelihood, no worry about getting one's bread, for that is provided regularly by others. One's person is protected by the Government. None of these things has to be paid for. By way of exercise, one gets ample work to do and, without any effort on one's part, all of one's bad habits fall away. The mind enjoys a sense of freedom. One has ready to hand the benefit of being absorbed in devotions to God. The body is held in bondage, but the soul grows more free. One is in full enjoyment of the use of one's limbs. The body is looked after by those who hold it in bondage. Thus, from every point of view, one is free. One might, perhaps, be in difficulties, be manhandled by a wicked warder, but then one learns to be patient.

One feels glad to have an opportunity of dissuading [him] from such behaviour. It is up to us to adopt such an attitude and think of gaol as a holy and happy place and to make it such. In short, happiness and misery are states of the mind.

I hope that the reader, after reading this account of my second experience [in Gaol], will resolve in his mind that his only happiness will be in going to gaol for the sake of the motherland or his religion, in submitting himself to the suffering involved in it, or bearing hardships in other ways.

(To be Continued)
[From Gujarati]

Indian Opinion, 30-1-1909

NOTE

1. *Vide* "Letter to A.H. West". 9-11-1908.

Part Three

MY THIRD EXPERIENCE IN GAOL

12
My Third Experience in Gaol–I

VOLKSRUST

When, on February 25, I was sentenced to three month's imprisonment with hard labour and I embraced my fellow-prisoners and my son in the Volksrust Gaol, I did not imagine that I would have much to say or write about this pilgrimage to gaol. But my expectation, like many other expectations of man, proved false. The experience I had this time was somethings new altogether. What I have learnt from this I would not have been able to learn even from years of study. I think these three months have been of inestimable value to me. In that brief period, I had many vivid experiences of *Satyagraha* and I think I am a better *Satyagrahi* today than I was three months ago. For all this, thanks are due to the local (the Transvaal) Government.

Some officers had sworn that I should in no circumstances get less than six months' imprisonment this time. My fellow-prisoners—elderly and prominent Indians—and my son—were all serving a six months 'term each, so that I wanted the officers' wish to be fulfilled.

However, since I had been charged under the Regulations framed under the Act,[1] I was afraid that three months would be the utmost I might get, and that is what happened.

After the sentence had been passed, it was a pleasure to join Mr. Dawad Mahomed, Mr. Rustomjee, Mr. Sorabji, Mr. Pillay, Mr. Hajurasingh, Mr. Lalbahadursingh and other veterans. Except ten of them, all were provided with beds in tents pitched on the ground in front of the gaol. The scene had therefore, the appearance of an armed camp rather than a Gaol. Everyone liked sleeping in a tent.

Arrangements for food were satisfactory. As on previous occasions, cooking was in our own hands. It was therefore, possible to prepare food to our taste. In all there were about 77 (*Satyagrahi*) prisoners.

Those who were taken outside for work were set a rather difficult task. They had to build a road in front of the magistrate's court. This required quarrying out stone, digging into heaps of stones that had been piled up, and carrying them in loads. After the work on the road was over, they were set to uproot the grass in the school compound.

But, on the whole, everyone worked cheerfully. I also went with the gangs for three days to join in this work. There was a telegram meanwhile that I should not be taken for work outside. I was rather disappointed, for I liked going out. It improved my health and kept me fit. Ordinarily, I have two meals a day, but on account of this exercise, the stomach insisted on my having three meals while in Volksrust Gaol. I was now assigned only the work of sweeping. That kind of work, I thought, would do me no good. And then came a time when I was denied even this.

WHY WAS I MADE TO LEAVE VOLKSRUST?

On March 2, I heard that my removal to Pretoria had been ordered. I was asked to get ready the same day. It was raining, the roads were bad; despite this, my warder and I were obliged to leave, with my luggage on my head. I was taken by the evening train the same day in a third-class carriage.

Some thought that this might possibly mean a settlement; others felt that the intention was probably to harass me by isolating me from the rest. Some also thought that the object might be to keep me in Pretoria and give me more freedom and better facilities so as to prevent a discussion in the House of Commons.

I did not like leaving Volksrust. Happy during the day, the evenings too we passed in cheerful conversation. Mr. Hajurasingh and Mr. Joshi, especially, asked a number of questions, which were in no way flippant, but were quite instructive. Which *Satyagrahi* would like to leave a place where conditions were so happy and where the largest number of Indians were congregated?

But man would not be man if things always happened as he wished. And so I left. On the way, Mr. Kajee saluted me. The warder and I found ourselves huddled up in a compartment. It was cold, and it rained the whole night. I had my overcoat with me, which I was allowed to put on. I felt a little better after that. I had been given bread and cheese to eat on the way. I did not touch them, since I had had my meal before starting. They were consumed by the warder.

IN PRETORIA GAOL

I reached Pretoria Gaol on the third. Everything appeared unfamiliar. Even the gaol is of recent construction. The men were strangers. They gave me something to eat, but I had no appetite. They placed before me mealie meal porridge; I tasted a spoonful, and left it off. The warder was surprised. I told him that I was not hungry. He smiled.

Then I passed on to the charge of another warder. He said: "Gandhi, take off your cap." I did so. He then asked me: "Are you Gandhi's son?" "No," I replied, "my son is serving six months in Volksrust."

I was then locked up in a cell. I began pacing up and down. Before long, the warder peeped through the watch-hole, saw what I was doing and shouted: "Gandhi, stop walking about like that: my floor is being spoiled." I stopped, and stood in a corner. I had nothing even to read.

I had not yet received my books. I must have been locked in at eight. At ten, I was taken to the physician. He asked me if I suffered from any contagious disease, and dismissed me. Was locked in again. At eleven, I was removed to another small cell. It was in this that I spent the rest of my term. It was a cell of the kind intended for one prisoner at a time. It measured, I believe, ten feet long and seven broad. The floor was covered with black pitch. The warders were constantly engaged in keeping it shining. For ventilation, it had a very small glass window, with iron bars. It was provided with an electric light for keeping a watch on the prisoner during the night. The light is not meant for the prisoner's use, for it is not powerful enough to read by.

Standing close to it, I could read a book printed in large type. The light is put out exactly at eight. But it is switched on five or six times in the night when the warders have a look at the prisoner through the watch-hole mentioned above.

After eleven, the Deputy-Governor came. I asked for three things from him: books, permission to write to my wife who was ill, and a small bench to sit on. As to the first, the reply was: "I shall see"; as to the second: "Yes"; as to the third: "No." When, however, I wrote in Gujarati, the letter was returned to me with the remarks that I should write in English. I said in reply that my wife did not know English, that my letters served as medicine for her, that they contained nothing of special significance. In spite of this, however, I did not get the permission. I refused to avail myself of the permission to write in English. The same evening my books were handed over to me.

When the mid-day meal arrived, I had to eat it in the cell standing, with the doors shut. At about three, I asked permission to take a bath. The soap for bathing must have been at a distance of about 125 feet. The warder replied: "All right. Undress (make yourself naked) and go." I asked him if this was necessary, suggesting that I could place my clothes on the screen. He then gave his permission, but asked me to be quick. While I had yet to wipe my body after bath, the gentleman shouted: "Are you ready, Gandhi?" I said I would not take long. I hardly ever got an opportunity to see an Indian face. When it was evening, I was given a blanket, with half a piece in addition, and a coir mat by way of bedding; there was no pillow or bed-board. Even when I went for evacuation, a warder stood by to keep watch. If by chance he did not know me, he would shout: "Sam, come out now." But Sam had the bad habit of taking a long time for evacuation; how could he get out so soon, and if he did, how would he feel easy in bowels afterwards? Sometimes a [white] warder, and sometimes a Kaffir, would thus stand by, and keep peeping over or shouting to the refrain of "Get up", "Get up".

The next day, I was given the work of polishing the floor and doors. The latter were made of varnished iron. What was the point of polishing them everyday? I have often spent three hours at a stretch on polishing one door. But I could not observe the slightest difference. Yes, it did make some difference to the floor. There were some Kaffirs working with me. They would sometimes talk in broken English of how they had come to be imprisoned, and ask me questions about my imprisonment. One asked me whether I had committed theft, and another whether I had been imprisoned for selling liquor. When I explained the correct position to one of the intelligent Kaffirs, he exclaimed, "Quite right." "*Amlungu bad*" (The whites are bad). "Don't pay fine." My cell bore the description "isolated". I saw five other cells adjoining mine bearing the same description. My neighbour was a Kaffir who had been serving a term of imprisonment for attempted murder. The three next to him were convicted of sodomy. It was in the company of such men and in such surroundings that I commenced my experience in Pretoria Gaol.

DIET

The food was in keeping with the conditions described above. Mealie pap in the morning, mealie pap with potatoes and carrots thrice a week for the mid-day meal, beans on other three days and rice without ghee for the evening meal. On Wednesdays, I received beans and rice with ghee for the mid-day meal, and on Sundays, rice and ghee with mealie pap. It was difficult to eat rice in the absence of ghee. I decided not to eat it till I was allowed ghee. The mealie pap served at breakfast and for the mid-day meal was sometimes not well cooked, and sometimes it was cooked so as to taste like *rab*[2]. The beans were only half-cooked sometimes, [though] generally they were good. On the days for vegetables, only four small potatoes [were served], which counted towards the [prescribed] eight ounces and, if it was the turn for carrots, only three, and these too rather small-sized.

Sometimes I would take four or five spoonfuls of mealie pap in the morning. But on the whole, I spent one and a half months on one meal of beans only at mid-day. My fellow-prisoners at Volksrust should realize from this how wrong they were to be angry with our own men when they did not sometimes cook well or when there was occasionally an insufficient supply of a particular item. One may be angry to some purpose, when our own friends attend to the cooking.

What could one do in the circumstances described above? It would be possible, of course, to express one's resentment. But

I think it would not be proper for us to make any such complaints. How can we complain when there are hundreds of prisoners who accept these things? A complaint must have only one object—to secure relief for other prisoners.

How would it mend matters if I were occasionally to complain to the warder about the small quantity of potatoes and so get him to serve me a little more? I once observed him giving me [an additional helping] from a portion meant for another, and thereafter gave up complaining altogether.

That no ghee was allowed with rice in the evening I knew before-hand, and I was determined to have the matter set right. I immediately brought it to the notice of the Chief Warder. He replied that ghee was allowed only with the mid-day meal on Wednesdays and Sundays in lieu of meat. He asked me to approach the physician if I wanted it oftener. The next day I asked for permission to see the physician. I was taken to him.

I asked him to order ghee for all Indian prisoners in lieu of fat. The Chief Warder was present. He said, "Gandhi's demand is not justified. Most of the Indians have been taking fat, and even meat. Those who refuse fat are given plain rice, which they readily accept. When there were *Satyagrahi* prisoners here, they also accepted it. They were weighed when entering and again when leaving the gaol. It was found that they all weighed more when leaving." The physician asked me, "Come on, now, what do you say to this?" I said I could not believe it. And speaking for myself, I said, I would certainly suffer in health if I had to go without ghee. The physician said that in that case he would order bread for me. I thanked him, but told him that I had not approached him specially for myself. So long as ghee was not ordered for everyone, I could not accept bread. Whereupon he said, "Please don't blame me now."

What was I to do now? If the Chief Warder had not intervened, ghee would have been ordered. The same day, I was offered bread and rice. I was hungry. But, as matters stood, how could a *Satyagrahi* accept the bread? I therefore, refused both. The next day I asked for permission to make a petition to the Director of Prisons which was granted.[3] In the petition, I cited the instances of Johannesburg and Volksrust [gaols] and asked for ghee to be ordered for all prisoners.

A reply to the petition was received after 15 days. It was to the effect that, pending the revision of the diet scale for Indians, I should be given ghee with rice everyday. Since, I did not know the exact terms of the order, I readily accepted rice, ghee and bread on the first day. I pointed out that there was no need for bread, but was told that it had been ordered by the physician and so would continue to be supplied.

Hence, I went on accepting that also for 15 days.[4] But my joy lasted no more than a day. I discovered the next day the terms of the order mentioned above, so that I again declined to accept rice, ghee and bread. I told the Chief Warder that I would not accept ghee so long as it was not ordered for every Indian. The Deputy-Governor, who was present, replied, "As you please."

I wrote again to the Director. I had been informed that the diet scale would be modified so as to bring it in line with the one in force in Natal. I expressed dissatisfaction with this and stated the reasons why I could not accept ghee. In the end, after more than a month and a half in all had elapsed, I was informed that ghee had been ordered for Indian prisoners wherever there was a large number of them [in one gaol]. It may thus be said that I broke the self-denial (*roza*) nearly a month and a half after I had taken up the matter. During nearly the whole of the concluding month [of my term of imprisonment], I took rice, ghee and bread, but went without a meal in the morning; and even after I had started taking rice and bread, whenever I was served mealie pap for the mid-day meal I would hardly take ten spoonfuls, fot it had a different taste everyday. The bread and ghee, however, stood me in good stead, and I was restored to health.

I have said above that I was restored to health, for it had broken down during the time that I lived on only one meal a day. I had lost my strength and had severe neuralgic pain in the head for ten days, and had also developed symptoms of some affection in the lungs.

CHANGE OF WORK

There was another reason why the lungs had been affected.

I said above that I was asked to polish the floor and doors. After ten days of this work, I was given two wornout blankets to be sewn into one. This was rather intricate work. It required me to bend down the whole day towards the floor, and that, too, while sitting in the cell. This used to give me backache by evening, and my eyes also began to feel the strain. Besides, I had all along believed that the air in the cell was unwholesome. Once or twice I asked the Chief Warder to give me some work outside, such as digging, etc. If that was not possible, I asked to be allowed to work on the blankets in the open air. He rejected both requests. I brought this matter also to the notice of the Director. In the end, the physician passed the [necessary] order and I was allowed to sew the blankets in the open air. If that had not been done, I think I would have suffered still more in health. There were some other difficulties after the order was passed, which it is not necessary to describe here. It so happened, therefore, that I got permission to work in the open air at about the same time that a change in my diet was ordered. The resulting gain was two-fold. When I was [first] given a blanket to sew, it was expected that it would take a week to finish it, so that, my entire term would be taken up with that work. But, contrary to expectations, after the first blanket had been finished, I could manage to sew a pair into one in two days. So, they found some other work for me, such as knitting a sweater, stitching purses for holding tickets, etc.

I had earlier told many *Satyagrahis* that, if anyone came out of gaol with impaired health, that would be a reflection on his spirit of *Satyagraha*, for it should be possible for us, given sufficient patience, to find remedies [for all difficulties in Gaol]. Moreover, one might suffer in health through worry. The *Satyagrahi* must learn to live in gaol as if it were a palace. Arguing thus, I used to feel anxious lest I myself should have to leave gaol in poor health. The reader must remember that I had suffered in health in the course of *Satyagraha* because I could not accept ghee which had been ordered for me alone. But this rule does not apply to others. Whenever, there is a single [Indian] prisoner in gaol, he can represent his own grievances for redress. In Pretoria I had a special reason for not doing so, and that is why

I was not in a position to accept ghee when ordered for me as a special case.

(To be continued)
[From Gujarati] *Indian Opinion, 29-5-1909*

NOTES

1. Gandhiji was charged with refusing to produce certificate of registration and to give finger-prints or other means of identification; *vide* 25-2-1909.
2. A liquid preparation of wheat flour boiled in water, generally for invalids.
3. *Vide* "Draft Petition to Gaol Governor", after 11-3-1909.
4. This is contradictory to the sentence which follows; *vide* also "Letter to the Press", 26-5-1909.

13
My Third Experience in Gaol–II

OTHER CHANGES

As I mentioned above, the warder in charge of me was somewhat harsh in his behaviour. This did not last long. When he saw that with the Government itself I took up a fighting attitude about food, etc., but carried out all his orders his manner changed, and I was allowed to do as I liked. Thus, the difficulties about lavatory, bath, etc., disappeared. Moreover, he never allowed me to feel that I was subject to his authority. His successor was a happy-go-lucky man. He was careful to provide me with all reasonable facilities. He used to say: "I love a man who fights for his people. I am myself something of a fighter. I do not regard you as a prisoner." Many a time he would console me with such talk.

Moreover, after a few days they used to let me out into the gaol yard for half an hour's stroll in the mornings and similarly, in the evenings. This exercise was continued even after I was allowed to sit outside for work. The rule about exercise applies to all prisoners who have to do work sitting.

And then the bench which had been refused to me was later sent by the Chief Warder of his own accord. Meanwhile, I received from General Smuts two books on religion, and I inferred from this that it was not under his orders that I had been subjected to hardships, but that it was the result of his negligence and that of others, as also a consequence of the fact that we are equated with the Kaffirs. One thing appeared certain, that the only object of isolating me was to see that I had no opportunity of talking to anyone. With some effort, I could also secure a pencil and a note book.

DIRECTOR'S VISIT

Within a few days of my being brought to Pretoria, Mr. Lichtenstein came to see me with special permission. He had come on official business, but he made inquiries about my health, etc. I was reluctant to give a reply, but, being pressed, I said to him: "Without going into details, I shall only say that I am being subjected to brutal treatment. General Smuts wants to bend me, but I am not likely to succumb. I am prepared to suffer everything. My mind is at peace.

Please do not make this public. I shall tell the world everything after my release". Mr. Lichtenstein conveyed this to Mr. Polak. The latter could not contain himself and talked about it to others. The result was that David Pollock wrote to Lord Selborne, and an inquiry was made.

There was a visit by the Director, to whom I said exactly what I had said to Lichtenstein. In addition, I also pointed out the other discomforts which I mentioned in the beginning. As a result of this, they sent me ten days later a bed board, a pillow, a night-shirt and a handkerchief. I accepted them. In the statement[1] which I have submitted on this matter, I have pointed out that all the Indians [in gaol] stand in need of these things. In fact, Indians are more comfort loving than whites in regard to sitting and sleeping. They find it difficult to do without a pillow.

Thus, simultaneously with improvement in diet and facilities for work in the open air, I was provided with better comfort for sleeping, as described above. But man can never escape his fate. The bed-board was full of bugs. I did not use it even for ten days. At last, the Chief Warder had it repaired and I started using it. Meanwhile, I had grown used to sleeping on a blanket spread out on the floor. The bed-board, therefore, appeared to have made no difference to me. In the absence of a pillow, I had been using my books for the purpose, so that even the provision of a pillow made little difference to me.

HANDCUFFED

The conclusion to which I had been led by my initial treatment [in Pretoria Gaol] was confirmed by the following incident. Four days later, I was summoned as a witness in Mrs. Pillay's case.

I was, accordingly, taken to the court. I was handcuffed on the occasion.[2]

Moreover, the warder locked up the handcuffs rather tight. I think he did this unintentionally. The Chief Warder saw this. I had obtained his permission to carry a book with me to read [on the way]. Thinking probably that I felt ashamed of the handcuffs, he asked me to hold the book with both hands, so that the handcuffs might not be seen. I was rather amused at this. To me the handcuffs were a matter of honour. It happened by chance that the title of the book which I was carrying, if rendered in Gujarati, would be: *Khuda-no Darbar Tara antar-man Chhe.*[3] I regarded this as a wonderful coincidence. Whatever, the difficulties that pressed on me from outside, so long as I kept my heart worthy of God's presence in it, what need had I to mind anything else? I was taken on foot in this fashion. For the return journey, a truck was sent from the Gaol. Indians must have come to know that I was to be brought [to the court]; some of them were, therefore, present there. From among them, Mr. Tryambaklal Vyas was able to see me through Mrs. Pillay's lawyer. I was also taken to the court on another occasion, this time, too, in handcuffs. There was a truck to carry us to the court as also to bring us back.

MAGIC POWER OF *SATYAGRAHA*

Some of the facts which I have given above will appear rather trivial, but they have been described in such detail in order to show that *Satyagraha* is feasible in every situation, serious or otherwise. The result of my having submitted to the physical hardships inflicted by the junior warder was that I could preserve my peace of mind. Not only that, the warders themselves removed all those hardships. If I had resisted, that would have distracted my energies from the bigger tasks on hand and the warders would have become my enemies.

On the question of food also, I remained firm in my principles and bore some hardships initially, with the result that this difficulty, too, disappeared. The same thing can also be seen [to have happened] in respect of the smaller difficulties.

The biggest gain, however, has been that I find myself, beyond any shadow of doubt, to have grown in mental strength in consequence of having endured physical suffering. I believe that the last three months have been of great profit to me and I am ready today to bear much heavier suffering without flinching. I see that *satyagraha* is assured of divine help, and that in testing a *satyagrahi* the Creator imposes on him at every step only as much burden as he can bear.

MY READING

The story of my suffering or of my happiness, or rather of both, ends here. But I had a great many benefits in the course of these three months. One of the most important, to be sure, was that I got an opportunity for reading. I must admit that, during the earlier part [of my imprisonment], I often found myself lost in thought and felt dejected. The moment I had succeeded in withdrawing my mind from an unpleasant thought, it would again wander off like a monkey. In such circumstances, men often go mad. My books saved me. Thanks to them, I did not feel much the absence of contacts with Indian friends. Everyday I had three hours for reading. I had an hour to myself in the morning, which could be spared [for reading] because I went without a breakfast. It was the same about evening. At noon, I read while eating. Besides, in the evening, I continued reading even after the light was switched on, if I was not too tired. On Saturdays and Sundays, I had plenty of time on land. I read over 30 books during this period, and reflected on some of them; among these, there were books in English, Hindi, Gujarati, Sanskrit and Tamil. Notable among the English books, I would say, were those by Tolstoy, Emerson and Carlyle. The first two were on religious subjects. Along with these, I also borrowed a copy of the *Bible* from the Gaol. Tolstoy's writings are so good and simple that a man belonging to any religion can profit by them. Moreover, he tries to put into practice what he preaches, so that, by and large, they command greater confidence.

There is a forceful book by Carlyle on the French Revolution. I realized after reading it that it is not from the white nations that India can learn the way out of her present degradation. It is my belief that the French people have gained nothing of value through the Revolution. Mazzini also thought the same way. There is much difference of opinion on this subject. We cannot enter into a discussion on it here. I came across many instances of *Satyagraha* even in this history.

The books in Gujarati, Hindi and Sanskrit which I read were *Veda-Shabda-Sangrah,* sent by Swamiji, the *Upanishads* received from Bhatt Keshavram, the *Manusmriti* received form Mr. Motilal Diwan, the *Ramayana* printed in Phoenix, *Patanjali-Yoga-Darshan, Ahnika-Prakasha* prepared by Nathuramji, and *Sandhya-ni Gutika,* given by Professor Parmanand, the *Gita* and the writings of the late worthy poet Raychand[4]. All of them gave me much food for thought.

The *Upanishads* proved a great source of peace to me. One statement in them has made a deep impression on my mind; in substance, it means that everything one does must be done for the welfare of the soul. The thought is expressed in words of great beauty. There is much else in it worthy of attention.

But it was the writings of the poet Raychand which proved the most satisfying. So far as I can judge, they should appeal to all. His way of life was noble, like Tolstoy's. I memorized a portion of his writings and of the book on *Sandhya*. I would repeat them over and over again in my mind whenever I happened to wake up at night, and every morning I spent half an hour meditating on them. I would recite most of what I had memorized, and this kept me cheerful all the time.

If ever I gave way to despair, I would smile with happiness again the moment I went back in thought to what I had read, and would be filled with gratitude to God. On this subject, too, I have a great many thoughts which I should like to place before the readers. But this is not the occasion to do so. I shall only say this, that in these days good books partly make up for the absence of good men with whom we can cultivate contacts, and that, therefore, every Indian who wants to be happy in gaol must form the habit of reading good books.

STUDY OF TAMIL

No other Indians can equal the performance of the Tamils in this fight. It, therefore, occurred to me that I should read Tamil with close attention, if for no other reason than to tender sincere thanks to them at least mentally. Accordingly, the last one month was devoted mostly to the study of Tamil. The more I learn it, the better I appreciate the beauties of this language. It is a very fine and sweet language, and from its structure and from what I have read in it, I find that the Tamils have produced, and still produce, a large number of intelligent, thoughtful and wise men. Moreover, since India is going to be one country, some Indians outside Madras should also learn Tamil.

CONCLUSION

I wish that everyone who reads this account of experience should cultivate patriotism, if he does not have it, and learn *Satyagraha* therefrom, and if he has it already, be more firm in it. I am growing more convinced everyday that no one who does not know his religion can have true patriotism in him.

For the rest—

The sky rings with the name of the Invisible, I sit rapt in the temple, my heart filled with gladness;

Taking up an *asana*[5], they face immovable, I have pitched my tent in the abode of the Inscrutable.

Moreover—

> Take to the life of a *fakir* and yield not to despondency,
> Let the mind be always rapt with joy.
> It is possible to practise renunciation while living in the world of men. And the last question is, how does one find *Khuda-Ishvar?*

The poet answers—

> When, smiling and playing my way through life,
> I see [Him] revealed to me, a visible presence,
> Then shall I consider my life to have attained its true end;
> He who has seen Him even in a dream,
> Will cease chasing the shadows in vain.

[From Gujarati]

Indian Opinion, 5-6-1909

NOTES

1. This is not available.
2. For official correspondence and other material on this subject, *vide* Appendix VIII.
3. *The Kingdom of God Is within You* by Tolstoy.
4. Also known as Rajachandra; *vide* "Letter to Maganlal Gandhi", 28-12-1908.
5. Yogic posture for contemplation.

14
My Jail Experiences–I[1]

The reader knows that I am a hardened criminal. It was not for the first time that I found myself a prisoner in the March of 1922. I had three previous South African convictions to my credit, and as I was regarded at the time by the South African Government as a dangerous criminal, I was moved from jail to jail and was able, therefore, to gather much experience of jail life.[2] I had, before the Indian conviction, passed through six prisons and had come in touch with as many Superintendents and many more jailors. When, therefore, during the beautiful night of the 10th of March I was taken to the Sabarmati Jail together with Mr. Banker, I did not feel any awkwardness which always attends upon a strange and new experience. I almost felt I was going from one home to another in order to make more conquests of love. The preliminaries were more like being taken to a pleasure-trip than to jail. The courteous Superintendent of Police, Mr. Healy, would not even enter the *Ashram*, but sent Anasuyabai with a message that he had a warrant for my arrest and that a car awaited me at the Ashram Gate. I was to take whatever time I needed for getting ready. Mr. Banker, who was on his way back to Ahmedabad, was met by Mr. Healy on the way and already arrested. I was not at all unprepared for the news that Anasuyabai brought. As a matter of fact, after having waited long enough for the coming of the warrant which everybody thought was imminent, I had given instructions that all should retire and I was myself about to lay myself to bed. I had returned that evening from Ajmer after a fatiguing journey where most reliable information was given to me that a warrant had been sent to Ajmer, for my arrest, but the authorities would not execute the warrant, as the very day that the warrant reached Ajmer, I was going back to Ahmedabad. The real news of the warrant, therefore, came as a welcome relief. I took with me an extra *kuchha* (lion-cloth), two blankets, and five books: *Bhagavad Gita*, *Ashram Hymn Book*, *Ramayana*, Rodwell's translation of the *Quran*, a presentation copy of the *Sermon on the Mount* sent by schoolboys of a high school in California with the hope that I would always carry it with me. The Superintendent, Khan Bahadur N.R. Wacha, received us kindly, and we were taken to a separate block of cells situated in a spacious, clean compound. We were permitted to sleep on the verandah of the cells, a rare privilege for prisoners. I enjoyed the quiet and the utter silence of the place. The next morning we were taken to the Court for preliminary examination. Both Mr. Banker and I had decided not only not to offer any defense, but in no way to hamper the prosecution, but rather to help it. The preliminary examination was, therefore, quickly over. The case was committed to the Sessions, and as we were prepared to accept short service, the trial was to take place on the 18th of March. The people of Ahmedabad had risen to the occasion. Mr. Vallabhhai Patel had issued strict instructions that there should be no crowds gathering near the Court-house and that there should be no demonstration of any kind whatsoever. There were, therefore, in the Court-house only a select body of visitors, and the police had an easy time of it, which I could see was duly appreciated by the authorities.

The week before the trial was passed in receiving visitors who were generally permitted to see us without restriction. We were allowed to carry on correspondence so long as it was harmless and submitted to the Superintendent. As we willingly carried out all the Jail regulations, our relations with the Jail officials were smooth and even cordial during the week that we were in Sabarmati. Khan Bahadur Wacha was all attention and politeness, but it was impossible not to notice his timidity in everything he did. He seemed to apologize for his Indian birth and unconsciously to convey that he would have done more for us had he been a European. Being an Indian, even in allowing facilities which the regulations permitted, he was afraid of the Collector and the Inspector-General of Prisons and every official who was at all superior to him. He knew that, if it came to a struggle between himself and the Collector or the Inspector-General of Prisons, he had nobody to back him up at the Secretariat. The notion of inferiority haunted him at every step. What was true outside was equally true, if not truer, inside the Jail. An Indian official would not assert himself, not because he could not, but because he lived in mortal fear of degradation, if not dismissal. If he was to retain his post and obtain promotion, he must please his superiors even to the point of ringer and even at the sacrifice of principles. The contrast became terrible when we were transferred to Yeravda. The European Superintendent had no fear of the Inspector-General of Prisons. He could claim just as much influence at the Secretariat as the latter. The Collector for him was almost an interloper. His Indian superiors he held cheap and, therefore, he was not afraid to do his duty when he wished and was equally unafraid to neglect it, when discharge of duty was an onerous task. He knew that, as a rule, he was always safe. This sense of safety enables young European officers often to do the right thing in spite of opposition either from the public or from the Government, and he has also often driven coach and six through all regulations, all instructions and defied public opinion.

Of the trial and the sentence I need say nothing as the reader knows all about it, except to acknowledge the courtesy which was extended to us by all the officials including the Judge and the Advocate-General. The wonderfull restraint that was observed by the small crowd of people that was seen in and about the Court, and the great affection showed by them can never be effaced from memory.

The sentence of six years' simple imprisonment I regarded as light. For, if Section 124A of the Penal Code did Really constitute [my action] a crime and the Judge administering the laws of the land could not but hold it as a crime, he would be perfectly justified in imposing the highest penalty. The crime was repeatedly and willfully committed, and I can only account for the lightness of the sentence by supposing not that the Judge took pity on me, for I asked for none, but that he could not have approved of Section 124 A. There are many instances of judges having signified their disapproval of particular laws by imposing the minimum sentence, even though the crime denoted by them might have been fully and deliberately committed.

He could not very well impose a lighter sentence seeing that the late Lokamanya was sentenced to six years' imprisonment for a similar offense.

The sentence over, we were both taken back to the prison, this time as fully convicted prisoners, but there was no change in the treatment accorded to us. Some friends were even permitted to accompany us. Leave-taking in the Jail was quite jovial. Mrs. Gandhi and Anasuyabai bore themselves bravely as they parted. Mr. Banker was laughing all the time and I heaved a sigh of relief, thanking God that all was over so peacefully and that I would be able to have some rest and still feel that I was serving the country, if possible more than when I was travelling up and down addressing huge audiences. I wish I could convince the workers that imprisonment of a comrade does not mean so much loss of work for a common cause. If we believe, as we have so often proclaimed we do, that unprovoked suffering is the surest way of remedying a wrong in regard to which the suffering is gone through, surely it follows as a matter of course that imprisonment of a comrade is no loss. Silent suffering undergone with dignity and humility speaks with an unrivalled eloquence. It is solid work because there is no ostentation about it. It is always true because there is no danger of miscalculation. Moreover, if we are true workers, the loss of a fellow-worker increases our zest and, therefore, capacity for work. And so long as we regard anybody as irreplaceable, we have not fitted ourselves for organized work. For organized work means capacity for carrying it on in spite of depletion in the ranks. Therefore, we must rejoice in the unmerited suffering of friends or ourselves and trust that the cause, if it is just, will prosper through such suffering.

Young India, 17-4-1924

NOTES

1. This was in reply to Kalicharan's telegram of April 16, 1924 which read: "Resolved to call All-India Depressed Classes Round Table Conference on 31st May – 1st June at Gondia through C.P. and Berar Depressed Classes Association's and earnestly request you alone to preside and decide all questions concerning us once for all."
2. For Gandhiji's earlier jail experiences; a condensed version appeared in *Young India*, 29-6-1922, 20-7-1922 and 10-8-1922.

15
My Jail Experiences–II

SOME OFFICIALS

It was on Saturday the 18th March that the trial was finished. We were looking forward to a quiet time in the Sabarmati Jail at least for some weeks. We had expected that the Government would not let us remain in that jail for any length of time. We were, however, not prepared for the very sudden removal that actually did take place.

For, the reader may recall that we were removed on Monday the 20th March to a special train which was to take us to the Yeravda Central Jail. We were made aware of the proposed removal only about an hour before departure. The officer-in-charge was all politeness and we were enabled to feel perfectly comfortable on the journey. But, immediately on alighting at Kirkee, we observed the difference and were made to feel that we were prisoners after all. The Collector and two others were awaiting the train. We were put in a motor prison-van which had perforations for ventilators. But for its hideous appearance, it could well be a *pardah* motor. Certainly, we could see nothing of the outside world. For the story of our reception at the Jail, the tearing away of Mr. Banker from me, his restoration, the first interview, and kindred interesting details, I must refer the reader to my letter[1] to Hakimji Ajmal Khan Saheb, already published in these columns. After the first unpleasantness, the relations between the then Superintendent, col. Dalziel, and ourselves rapidly improved. He was most considerate regarding our creature comforts. But there was a certain something about him which always jarred. He would never forget that he was Superintendent and we were prisoners. He would not let it be granted that we were fully aware that we were prisoners and he was Superintendent. I made bold to say that we never once forgot that we were prisoners. We showed him all the deference due to his rank. The reminders were so unnecessary. But he had the needlessly haughty demeanour which one often regretfully notices about so many British officials. This weakness of his made him distrustful of the prisoners. Let me give a pleasant illustration of what I mean. He was most anxious that I should eat more than I was taking.

He wanted me to take butter. I told him I could take only goat's milk butter. He gave special orders that it should be procured at once. Well, it came. The difficulty was what to mix it with. I suggested that some flour might be issued to me. It was given. But it was too coarse for my very delicate digestive apparatus. Refined mill flour was ordered and 20 lbs. was issued to me. What was I to do with all this? I cooked or Mr. Banker cooked for me *chapatis*. After some trial, I felt I needed neither flour nor butter. I asked that the flour may be removed from me and the issue of butter stopped. Col. Dalziel would not listen. What was issued was issued. I might feel tempted later. I pleaded that it was all waste of public money. I gently suggested that, I was as solicitous about the use of public money as I would be about my own. There was an incredulous smile. I then I said, "Surely, it is my money." "How much have you contributed to the public treasury?" was the quick retort. I humbly replied, "You contribute only a percentage out of the salary you get from the State, whereas, I give the whole of myself, labour, intelligence and all." There was a loud burst of suggestive laughter. But I did not collapse for I believed what I said. A labourer like me who labours for the State for mere maintenance contributes more to the State than a Viceroy who receives Rs. 20,000 together with royal residencies and contributes to the State, if his salary be not income-tax-free, a certain percentage of his salary. It becomes possible for him and those who belong to the system of which he is the chief to receive what he does out of the labour of millions. And yet many Englishmen and some Indians honestly believe that they serve the State (whatever, the word may mean to them) more than the labourers and, in addition, contribute from their very salaries a percentage towards the upkeep of the State. There never was a grosser fallacy or a more absurd presumption than this modern belief in selfrighteousness.

But I must return to the gallant Colonel. I have given the pleasantest sample of Col. Dalziel's haughty distrust. Will the reader believe that I had to carefully preserve the flour till the advent of Major Jones who took Col. Dalziel's place when the latter acted for the Inspector-General of Prison?

Major Jones was the very reverse of Col. Dalziel. From the very first day of his arrival, he became friends with the prisoners. I have a vivid recollection of our first meeting. Although he came with Co.

Dalziel with becoming ceremonial, there was a refreshing absence of officialdom about him. He greeted me familiarly and talked about my fellow-prisoners in Sabarmati and conveyed their regards too, which he said they had sent. Though a strict disciplinarian, he never stood on his dignity. I have rarely met an official, whether European or Indian, so free from humbug or false notions of prestige and dignity. He was ready to confess errors—a dangerous and rare practice with Government officials. He once awarded punishment not to a 'political' prisoner, but to a helpless *bona-fide* criminal. He subsequently came to learn that the punishment was not deserved. He straightway and without any pressure from outside cancelled it and made the following remarkable entry: 'I repent for my decision' in the prisoner's history ticket. the accurate manner in which the prisoners sum up superintendents is truly amazing. Major Jones was *bahot bhala*[2]. They had nicknames for every one of the officials.

To finish, however, the story of my attempt to save the flour and other superfluous articles of diet. At Major Jones's very first visit of inspection I requested that what I did not need should be cut off. He immediately gave orders that my request should be complied with.

Col. Dalziel distrusted my motives; his successor took me at my word and he allowed me to make all the changes I wanted in the interest of economy, never once suspecting that I could be guilty of mental reservations. Another official with whom we early came in contact was, of course, the Inspector-General of Prisons. He was stiff, monosyllabic and gave one the impression that he was severe. His reserve was peculiarly his own and most uncomfortable for poor prisoners. Most officials being deficient in imagination often do unintentional injustices. They refuse to see the other side. They will not have patience to listen to prisoners and expecting from them prompt, coherent replies, and failing to get them, succeed in giving wrong decisions. Visits of inspection are often, therefore, a farce and almost invariably result in the wrong men-bullies or sycophants-being favoured. The right man, the silent humble prisoner will not be heard.

Indeed, most of the officials frankly admit that their duty is confined to keeping the prisoners sanitarily clean, preventing prisoners from fighting one another or from absconding and keeping them healthy.

I must consider in the next chapter one of the sad results of this mentality.

Young India, 24-4-1924

NOTES

1. *Vide* "Letter to Hakim Ajmal Khan", 14-4-1922.
2. Very good.

16
My Jail Experiences–III

SOME TERRIBLE RESULTS

In this chapter, I propose to discuss the results of the officials thinking that their duty ends with caring for the health of the prisoners, preventing fights among them or absconding. I do not think I am exaggerating when I say that jails may be described as well- or ill-managed cattle-farms. A Superintendent who ensures good food for the prisoners and does not punish without cause is considered both by the Government and the prisoners as a model Superintendent. Neither party expects more. If a Superintendent were to introduce the real human touch in his relations with the prisoners, he is highly likely to be misunderstood by the prisoners and will very probably be distrusted by the Government as being unpractical, if not worse.

The jails have, therefore, become hot beds of vice and degradation.

The prisoners do not become better for their life in them. In most cases they become worse than before. Perhaps all the world over, the jails are an institution the most neglected by the public. The result is that there is little or no public check on their administration. It is only when a political prisoner of some fame finds himself within the walls of a prison that there is any public curiosity about the happenings therein.

What classification there is of prisoners is regulated more in the interest of the administration than those of the prisoners. Thus, for instance, one would find habitual criminals and persons who have committed not a moral but a merely statutory offence are put together in the same yard, in the same block and even in the same cell. Fancy forty or fifty persons of varying types being locked in the same cell for night after night! An educated man, who had been convicted under the Stamp Act for having used an officially-defaced stamp, was put in the same block as habitual offenders regarded as dangerous characters. It is no unusual thing to see murderers, abductors, thieves and mere statutory offenders huddled together. There are some tasks which can only be done jointly by several men, such as working the pump. Able-bodied men alone can be put onto such tasks. Some highly sensitive men were included in one such gang. Now the ordinary prisoners in such a gang will use language which no decent man would care to hear. The men who use indecent language have no sense of indecency in the language they use. But a sensitive man will feel most uncomfortable when such language is used in his presence.

Convict-warders are in immediate charge of such gangs. In the discharge of their duty, it is customary for them to swear at prisoners in the choicest billings gate. And when they are sufficiently worked up, they do not spare the rod either. Needless to say, both the punishments are not only unauthorised, but they are unlawful. I could however, present quite a decent catalogue of things unlawful that happen in jails to the knowledge of, and sometimes even with the connivance of officials. In the case mentioned by me, the sensitive prisoner could not put up with the foul language. He, therefore, refused to work in the gang unless it was stopped. It was due to the prompt intervention of Major Jones that a most awkward situation was averted. But the relief was momentary. He had no power to stop a recurrence of the trouble; for it must continue to recur so long as prisoners are not classified in accordance with a moral standard and with regard to their human requirements rather than administrative convenience.

One would have thought that, in a jail where every prisoner is under surveillance night and day and can never be out of the sight of a warder, crimes will not be possible. But, unfortunately, every conceivable crime against morality is not only possible, but is committed almost with impunity. I need not mention small pilferings, deceptions, petty and even serious assaults, but I wish to refer to unnatural crimes. I will not shock the reader with any details. In spite of my many jail experiences, I did not think that such crimes were possible in jails. But the Yeravda experience gave me more than one painful shock. The discovery of the existence of unnatural crimes produced one of the greatest of the shocks. All the officials who spoke to me about them said that, under the existing system, it was impossible to prevent them. Let the reader understand that, in a majority of cases, the consent of the victim is lacking. It is my deliberate opinion that it is possible to prevent such crimes if the administration of jails is humanized and can be made a matter of public concern. The number of prisoners in the jails of India must be several hundred thousand. It should be the concern of public workers to know what happens to them. After all, the motive behind punishment is reformation. The legislature, the judge and the jailor are believed to expect that the punishments would act as deterrents, not merely for the physical and mental hurt they cause, but for the repentance that prolonged isolation must bring about. But the fact is that punishments only brutalize the prisoners. In the jails they are never given an opportunity for repentance and reform. The human touch is lacking. True, there is a weekly visit from religious preachers.

I was not permitted to attend any of these meetings, but I know that they are mostly shams. I do not wish to suggest that the preachers are shams. But a religious service once a week for a few minutes can produce no impression on those who ordinarily see nothing wrong in crimes. It is necessary to provide a responsive atmosphere in which a prisoner unconsciously sheds bad and cultivates good habits.

But such atmosphere is impossible so long as the system of entrusting convicts with most responsible work is continued. By far the worst part of the system is the appointment of convict-officers.

These men are necessarily long-term prisoners. They are, therefore, men who have committed the most serious crimes. Generally, the bullies are chosen as warders. They are the most forward. They succeed in pushing themselves to the front. They are the instruments for the commission of almost all the crimes that take place in the jails. A free fight resulting in one death once took place because two such warders were concerned in the same prisoner who was a victim of their unnatural lust. Everyone knew what was happening in the jail.

But the authorities intervened only to prevent further fighting and further bloodshed. These convict-officers recommend tasks for the other prisoners. They supervise the tasks. They are responsible for the good behaviour of the prisoners under their charge. In fact, the will of the permanent officers is expressed and carried out through these convicts who are dignified as "officers". The marvel to me was that under such a system, things were not much worse than they actually were. It once more demonstrated to me how superior men were to a wicked system as they were inferior to a good one. Human beings seem naturally to seek the middle path.

The whole of the cooking, too, is entrusted to prisoners. The result is indifferent cooking and organized favouritism. It is the prisoners who grind corn, shred vegetables, cook food and serve.

When complaints as to short and badly cooked rations were recurringly made, the invariable answer was that the remedy was in their own hands as they cooked their own food, as if they were related to one another and understood mutual responsibility! Once when I pushed the argument to its logical extent, I was told that no administration could afford the cost. I differed from the view at the time of argument. Further observation has confirmed me in my contention that, under a well-devised system, jail administration can be made self-supporting.

I hope to devote a chapter to an examination of jail economics. For the present, I must satisfy myself with saying that no question of cost can possibly be admitted as relevant in a consideration of moral abuses.

Young India, 1-5-1924

17
My Jail Experiences–IV[1]

'POLITICAL' PRISONERS

"We do not make any distinction between political and other prisoners. Surely you do not want any such distinction to be made in your favour?" Thus said Sir George Lloyd[2] when he visited the Yeravda Jail about the end of the last year. He said that in reply to an inadvertent use made by me of the adjective 'political'. I ought to have known better. For I was fully aware of the Governor's distaste for that word. And yet, strange to say, the history tickets of most of us were marked 'political'. When I remarked upon the anomaly, I was told by the then Superintendent that the distinction was private and was intended only for the guidance of the authorities. We, the prisoners, were to ignore it, for we could not base any claim upon it.

I have reproduced Sir George Lloyd's language word for word so far as I can remember. There is a sting about what Sir George[3] Lloyd said. And it was so gratuitous. For he knew that I was asking for no favours and no distinction. Circumstances had[4] brought about a general discussion. But the idea was to tell me, "You are no better than the rest in the eye of the law and the administration." And yet the painful inconsistency was that the very time that the distinction was, without any occasion for it, combated in theory, it was made in practice. Only, in the majority of Gases, it was made against the political prisoners.

As a matter of fact, it is impossible to avoid making distinctions.

If the human factor were not ignored, it would be necessary to understand a prisoner's habits of life, and model his life accordingly in the prisons. It is not a question of distinguishing between rich men and poor men or educated and uneducated, but between modes of life these antecedents have developed in them. As against the inevitable recognition of the existing fact, it has been urged that the men who commit crimes should know that the law is no respecter of persons, and that it is the same to the law whether a rich man or a graduate or a labourer commits theft. This is a perversion of a sound law. If it is really the same to the law as it should be, each will get the treatment according to his capacity for suffering. To give thirty stripes to a delicately-built thief and as many to an able-bodied one would be not impartiality but vindictiveness towards the delicate one and probably indulgence to the able-bodied. Similarly to expect, say, Pandit Motilalji[5] to sleep on a rough coirmat spread on hard floor is additional punishment, not equality of treatment.

If the human factor was introduced into the administration of the jails, the ceremony on admission would be different from what it is today. Finger-impressions would undoubtedly be taken, a record of past offences would find its place in the register. But there will be, in addition, particulars about the prisoner's habits and mode of life. Not distinction but classification is perhaps the word that better describes the necessary method which the authorities, if they would treat prisoners as human beings, must recognize. Some kind of classification there already is. For instance, there are circles wherein prisoners are housed in batches in long cells. Then there are the separate single cells intended for dangerous criminals. There are solitary cells where prisoners undergoing solitary confinement are locked. There are, again, the condemned cells in which are locked prisoners awaiting the gallows. Lastly, there are cells for under-trial prisoners. The reader will be surprised to find that political prisoners were mostly confined in the separate division or the solitary. In some cases, they were confined in condemned cells. Let me not do an injustice to the authorities. Those who do not know these divisions and cells may form the impression that the condemned cells, for instance, must be specially bad. Such, however, is not the case. The cells are all well-constructed and airy so far as

Yeravda Jail is concerned. What is, however, open to strong objection is the association about these cells.

The classification being, as I have shown, inevitable and in existence, there is no reason why it should not be scientific and human. I know that revision of classification according to my suggestion means a revolution in the whole system. It undoubtedly means more expense and a different type of men to work the new system. But additional expense will mean economy in the long run.

The greatest advantage of the proposed revolution would no doubt be a reduction in the crimes and reformation of the prisoners. The jails would then be reformatories representing to society sinners as its reformed and respectable members. This may be a far-off event. If we were not under the spell of a long-lived custom, we should not find it a difficult task to turn our prisons into reformatories.

Let me quote here a pregnant remark made by one of the jailors. He once said:

> "When I admit search or report prisoners, I often ask myself whether I am a better man than most of them. God knows I have been guilty of worse crimes than what some have come here for. The difference is that these poor men have been detected whereas I am not."

Is not what the good jailor confessed true of many of us? Is it not true that there are more undetected than detected crimes? Society does not point the finger of scorn at them. But habit has made us look askance at those who are not smart enough to escape detection.

Imprisonment often makes them hardened criminals.

The animal treatment commences on arrest. The accused are in theory assumed to be innocent unless they are found guilty. In practice the demeanour of those in charge of them is one of haughtiness and contempt. A convicted man is lost to society. The atmosphere in the prison inures him to the position of inferiority.

The political prisoners do not as a rule succumb to this debilitating atmosphere, because they, instead of responding to the depressing atmosphere, act against it and, therefore, even refine it to a certain extent. Society, too, refuses to regard them as criminals. On the contrary, they become heroes and martyrs. Their sufferings in the jail are exaggerated by the public. And such indulgence in many cases even demoralizes the political prisoners. But unfortunately, exactly in proportion to the indulgence of the public, is the strictness, mostly unwarranted, of the officials. The Government regard the political prisoners as more dangerous to society than the ordinary prisoner. An official seriously contended that a political prisoner's crime placed the whole society in danger whereas an ordinary crime harmed only the criminal.

Another official told me that the reason why the political prisoners were isolated and denied newspapers, magazines, etc., was to bring the guilt home to them. Political prisoners, he said, seemed to glory in 'imprisonment'. The deprivation of the liberty, while it afflicted the ordinary criminal, left the political prisoner unmoved. It was, therefore, he added, but natural that the Government should devise some other method of punishment. hence, he said, the denial of facilities which otherwise such prisoners should undoubtedly have.

The remarks were made in connection with my request for *The Times of India* weekly, or the *Indian Social Reformer,* or the *Servant India* or *Modern Review* or *Indian Review.* Let the reader not regard this deprivation as a light penalty for those who regard the newspaper as a necessity in no way inferior to breakfast. I dare say that Mr. Majli would not have suffered mental derangement If he had been allowed the use of newspapers[6]. It is equally depressing for one who is not, like me, a reformer for all occasions, to be put up together with dangerous criminals as almost all the political prisoners were put in Yeravda. It is no light thing to be in the company of those who never speak but to utter foul language or whose conversation is as a rule indecent. I could understand political prisoners being put in such surroundings, if the Government sanely took them in their confidence and used them to exercise a wholesome influence on the ordinary criminal. This, however is, I admit, not a practical proposition. My contention is that placing of political prisoners in unwholesome surroundings is an additional and an unwarranted punishment. They ought to be put in a separate division and given a treatment in keeping with their antecedents.

I hope civil resisters will not misunderstand this or any other chapter in which I have advocated reforms of prisons. It would ill become a civil resister to resent whatever inconvenience he may be subjected to. He is out to put up with the roughest treatment. If the treatment is humane, it is well; but it is also well if it be otherwise.

Young India, *8-5-1924*

NOTES

1. For the first three articles of this series.
2. Governor of Bombay; for Gandhiji's letter to him regarding prisoner classification, *vide* "Letter to Governor of Bombay", 15-8-1923.
3. The message, given by Gandhiji before leaving the Sessions Court, Ahmedabad, on being sentenced, should be read with "Message to the Country"; *vide* 18-3-1922.
4. The source has "has".
5. Motilal Nehru (1861-1331), prominent lawyer and Swarajist leader; President, Indian National Congress, 1919 and 1928.
6. *Vide* "Notes", 3-4-1924.

18
My Jail Experiences–V

POSSIBILITIES OF REFORM

It has been my invariable experience that good evokes good, evil—evil; and that therefore, if the evil does not receive the corresponding response, it ceases to act, dies of want of nutrition. Evil can only live upon itself. Sages of old, knowing this law, instead of returning evil for evil, deliberately returned good for evil and killed it.

Evil lives nevertheless, because many have not taken advantage of the discovery, though the law underlying it acts with scientific precision. We are too lazy to work out in terms of the law the problems that face us and, therefore, fancy that we are too weak to act up to it. The fact is, that the moment the truth of the law is realized, nothing is so easy as to return good for evil. It is the one quality that distinguishes man from the brute. It is man's natural law not to retaliate. Though we have the human form, we are not truly human till we have fully realized the truth of the law and acted up to it. The law admits of no escape.

I cannot recall a single instance in which it has not answered. Utter strangers have within my experience irresistibly responded to it. In all the South African jails through which I passed, the officials who were at first most unfriendly to me became uniformly friendly because I did not retaliate. I answered their bitterness with sweetness.

This does not mean that I did not fight injustice. On the contrary, my South African jail experiences were a continuous fight against it, and in most cases it was successful. The longer Indian experience has but emphasized the truth and the beauty of non-violent conduct. It was the easiest thing for me to acerbate the authorities at Yeravda. For instance, I could have answered the Superintendent in his own coin when he made the insulting remarks described in my letter to Hakim Saheb.[1] I would have in that case lowered myself in my own estimation and confirmed the Superintendent in his suspicion that I was a cantankerous and mischievous politician. But the experiences related in that letter were trivialities compared to what was to follow.

Let me recall a few of them.

A European warder I knew suspected me. He thought it was his business to suspect every prisoner. As I did not want to do any the slightest thing without the knowledge of the Superintendent, I had told him that, if a prisoner passing by salaamed, I would return the *salaam* and that I was giving to the convict-warder in charge of me all the food that I could not eat. The European warder knew nothing of the conversation with the Superintendent. He once saw a prisoner salaam me. I returned the salaam. He saw us both in the act, but only took from the prisoner his ticket. It meant that the poor man would be reported. I at once told the warder to report me too, as I was equally guilty with the poor man. He simply told me he had to do his duty.

Instead of reporting the warder for his officiousness, but in order to protect a fellow-prisoner, I merely mentioned to the Superintendent the incident of salaaming without the conversation I had with the warder. The latter recognized that I meant no ill whatsoever to him, and from that time forward ceased to suspect me. On the contrary, he became very friendly.

I was subject to search like the other prisoners. I never objected. And so, daily before the lock-up, a regular search took place for many months. Occasionally, a jailor used to come who was exceptionally rude. I had nothing but my loin-cloth on. There was, therefore, no occasion for him to touch my person. But he did touch the groins. Then he began overhauling the blankets and other things. He touched my pot with his boots. All this was proving too much for me and my anger was about to get the better of me. Fortunately, I regained self-possession and said nothing to the young jailor. The question, however, still remained whether I should or should not report him. This happened a fairly long time after my admission to Yeravda. The Superintendent was, therefore, likely to take severe notice of the jailor's conduct if I reported him. I decided to the contrary. I felt that I must pocket these personal rudenesses. If I reported him, the jailor was likely to lose his job. Instead, therefore, of reporting him, I had a talk with him. I told him how I had felt his rudeness, how I had at first thought of reporting him and how in the end I decided merely to talk to him. He took my conversation in good part and felt grateful. He admitted, too, that his conduct was wrong, though he said he did not act with the intention of wounding my susceptibilities. He certainly never molested me again. Whether he improved his general conduct in regard to other prisoners I do not know.

But what was most striking was perhaps the result of my intervention in connection with the floggings and the hunger-strikes.

The first hunger-strike was that of the Sikh life-sentence prisoners. They would not eat food without the restoration of their sacred loin-cloth and without the permission to them to cook their own food.

As soon as I came to know of these strikes, I asked to be allowed to meet them. But the permission could not be granted. It was a question of prestige and jail discipline. As a matter of fact, there was no question of either, if the prisoners could be regarded as human beings Just as susceptible to finer forces as their species outside. My seeing them, I feel sure, would have saved the authorities a great deal of trouble worry and public expense, and would also have saved the Sikh prisoners the painful, prolonged fast But, I was told, if I could not see them, I could send them 'wireless messages'! I must explain this special expression. Wireless messages in prison parlance means unauthorized messages sent by one prisoner to another with or without the knowledge of the officials. Every official knows and must connive at such interchange of messages. Experience has shown them that it is impossible to guard against or to detect such breaches of prison regulations. I may say that I was scrupulously exact about such messages. I cannot recall a single occasion when I sent a 'wireless' for my own purpose. In every case it was in the interest of prison discipline. The result was,

I think, that the officials had ceased to distrust me and, if they had it in their power, they would have availed themselves of my offer of intervention in such cases. But the superior authority, so jealous of its prestige, would not hear of it.

In the above instance, I did set in motion the wireless apparatus, but it was hardly effective. The fast was broken after many days, but I am unable to say whether it was at all due to my messages.

This was the first occasion when I felt that I should intervene in the interest of humanity.

The next occasion was when certain Mulshi Peta prisoners were flogged for short task.[2] I need not go into the painful story at length.

Some of these prisoners were youngsters. It is likely that they had wilfully done much less task than they could have. They were put on grinding. Somehow or other these prisoners were not classed political as the *Swaraj* prisoners were. Whatever the cause, they were mostly given grinding as their task. Grinding has an unnecessary bad odour about it. I am aware that all labour is irksome when it has to be done as a task and under supervision not always gentle. But a prisoner who courts imprisonment for conscience sake should look upon his task as a matter of pride and pleasure. He should put his whole soul into the labour that may be allotted to him. The Mulshi Peta prisoners, or for that matter the others, as a body were certainly not of this type. It was a new experience for them all and they did not know what was their duty as *Satyagrahis*—whether to do the most or the least or not at all.

The majority of the Mulshi Peta prisoners were perhaps indifferent. They had perhaps not given a thought to the thing. But they were mostly high-spirited men and youths. They would brook no *jo hukum* and, therefore, there was constant friction between them and the officials.

The crisis came at last. Major Jones became angry. He thought they were wilfully not doing their task. He wanted to make an example of them and ordered six of them to receive stripes. The flogging created a sensation in the prison. Everybody knew what was happening and why. I noticed the prisoners as they were passing by. I was deeply touched. One of them recognized me and bowed. In the 'separate', the 'political' prisoners intended to strike as a protest. I have paid my tribute to Major Jones. Here, it is my painful duty to criticize his action. In spite of his sterling good nature, love of justice and even partiality for prisoners as against officials, he was hasty in action. His decisions were sometimes, therefore, erroneous. It would not matter, as he is equally ready to repent, if it was not for sentences like flogging which once administered are beyond recall. I discussed the matter gently with him, but I know that I could not persuade him that he was wrong in punishing prisoners for short task. I could not persuade him to think that every short task was not proof of wilfulness. He did indeed admit that there always was a margin fear error, but his experience was that it was negligible. Unfortunately, like so many officers, he believed in the efficacy of flogging.

The political prisoners, having taken a serious view of the case, were on the point of hunger-striking. I came to know of it.[3] I felt that it was wrong to hunger-strike without an overwhelming case being made out. The prisoners could not take the law into their own hands and claim to judge every case for themselves. I asked Major Jones again for permission to see them. But that was not to be allowed. I have already published the correspondence[3] on the subject which I invite the studious reader to consult at the time of reading these notes. I had, therefore, again to fall back upon the 'wireless'. The hunger strike and a crisis were averted as a direct result of the 'wireless'. But there was an unpleasant incident arising from the matter. Mr. Jeramdas[4] had delivered my message contrary to the regulations. Mr. Jeramdas saw, as he had to see, the political prisoners concerned. They were purposely kept in separate blocks. He, therefore, 'wandered' from his own to the other blocks with the knowledge of the convict officers and one of the European jailors. He told them that he knew that he was breaking the regulations and that they were free to report him. He was reported in due course. Major Jones thought that he could not but take notice of the breach although he knew that it was for a good cause, and although he even appreciated Mr. Jeramdas's work. The punishment awarded was seven days' solitary confinement.

On my coming to know of this, I invited Major Jones to award at least the same penalty to me as to Mr. Jeramdas. For he (Mr. Jeramdas) had broken the regulations at my instance. Major Jones said that in the interest of discipline he was bound to take notice of an open defiance brought officially to his notice. But he was not only not displeased with what Mr. Jeramdas had done, but he was glad that, even at the risk of being punished, he saw the prisoners who were about to hunger strike and thus saved an ugly situation. There was no occasion, he saw, to punish me as I had not left my boundary and as my instigation of Mr. Jeramdas was not officially brought to his notice. I recognized the force of Major Jones's argument and attitude and did not further press for punishment.

I must consider in the next chapter another incident still more telling and important from the *Satyagrahi* standpoint and then consider the moral results of non-violent action and the ethics of fasting.

Young India, 15-5-1924

NOTES

1. *Vide* "Letter to Hakim Ajmal Khan", 14-4-1922.
2. *Vide* "Letter to Major W. Jones", 10-2-1923.
3. The reference is to the letters addressed by Gandhiji to the Superintendent, Yeravda Jail, and the Governor of Bombay. For these letters along with Gandhiji's notes thereon. published in *Young India,* 6-3-1924.
4. Jairamdas Doulatram (*b.* 1892); Secretary, Sind Provincial Congress Committee; later became Minister of Food and Agriculture, Government of India; Governor of Bihar and Assam.

19
My Jail Experience–VI

ETHICS OF FASTING

When the incidents related in the Last chapter took place, my cell was situated in a triangular block containing eleven tells. They were also part of the separate division, but the block was separated from the other separate blocks by a high massive wall. The base of the triangle lay alongside the road leading to the other separate blocks.

Hence, I was able to watch and see the prisoners that passed to and fro. In fact, there was constant traffic along the road. Communication with the prisoners was therefore easy. Some time after the flogging incident, we were removed to the European yard. The cells were better ventilated and more roomy. There was a pleasant garden in front. But we were more secluded and cut off from all contact with the prisoners whom we used to see whilst we were in the 'separate'. I did not mind it. On the contrary, the greater seclusion gave me more time for contemplation and study. And the 'wireless' remained intact. It was impossible to prevent it so long as it was necessary for a single other prisoner or official to see us. In spite of effort to the contrary, someone of them would drop a remark resulting in our knowing the happenings in the jail. So one fine morning we heard that several Mulshi Peta prisoners were flogged for short task and that, as a protest against the punishment, many other Mulshi Peta prisoners had commenced a hunger strike. Two of these were well known to me.

One was Dev and the other Dastane. Mr. Dev had worked with me in Champaran, and had proved one of the most conscientious, sober and honest among the co-workers whom I had the privilege of having in Champaran. Mr. Dastane of Bhusaval is known to everybody. The reader may therefore, imagine my pain when I heard that Dev was among the party flogged and that he was also one of the hunger strikers.

Messrs Indulal Yagnik[1] and Manzar Ali Sokta were at this time my fellow-prisoners. They were agitated equally with me. Their first thought was to declare a sympathetic hunger-strike. We discussed the propriety of such a strike and came to the conclusion that it would be wrong to do so. We were neither morally nor in any other way responsible for the floggings or the subsequent hunger-strike. As *Satyagrahis* we were to be prepared for and to suffer cheerfully the rigours of jail life and even injustices including flogging. Such hunger-strike, therefore, with a view to preventing future punishment would be a species of violence done to the jail officials. Moreover, we had no right to sit in judgment upon the action of the authorities. That would be an end to all prison discipline. And even if we wished to judge the authorities, we had not and could not get sufficient data to warrant an impartial judgment. If the fast was to be out of sympathy with the hunger-strikers, we had no data to enable us to judge whether their action was justified or not. Any one of these grounds was sufficient to show that the proposed fast would be wholly premature.

But I suggested to my friends that I should try to find out the true facts through the Superintendent, and endeavour as before to get into touch with the hunger-strikers. I felt that we as human beings could not possibly remain uninterested in such matters although we were prisoners, and that under certain circumstances even a prisoner was entitled to claim a hearing in the matter of general jail administration when it was likely to result in the perpetration of gross injustice bordering on inhumanity. So, we all decided that I should approach the authorities in the matter. The letter of 29th June, 1923[2], published in *Young India* of March 6, 1924, will give the reader further details about the matter. There was a great deal of correspondence and negotiation which, being of a confidential nature, I do not wish to publish. I can however say that the Government recognized that I had no desire to interfere with the prison administration and that my proposal to be permitted to see the two leaders among the hunger-strikers was dictated by purely humanitarian motives. They, therefore, permitted me to see Messrs Dastane and Dev in the presence of the Superintendent and Mr. Griffiths, the Inspector-General of Police.

It was to me a rare pleasure and a matter of pride to see these two friends walking unaided and with a steady step after full thirteen days' unbroken fast. They were as cheerful as they were brave. I could see that they were terribly reduced in body, but their spirit had waxed strong in exact proportion to the reduction of the body. As I hugged them and greeted them with the question, "Are you nearly dead?" they rang out, "Certainly not," and Dastane added, "We are able to prolong the fast indefinitely, if need be, for we are in the right." "But if you are in the wrong?" I asked. "We shall then like men admit our mistake and abandon the fast," was the reply. By their brightness they made me forget that they were suffering from pangs of hunger. I wish I had leisure to reproduce the whole of the ethical discourse we held.

Their ground for fasting was that the punishment inflicted by the Superintendent was unjust and that, therefore, unless the Superintendent admitted his mistake and apologized, they must go on with the fast. I pleaded that this was not a correct attitude. Whilst I was discussing the moral basis of their action, the Superintendent voluntarily and out of his usual good nature intervened and said, "I tell you, if I felt that I had done wrong, I should surely apologize. I know that I do make mistakes. We all do. I may have erred even in this case, but I am not conscious of it." I continued my pleading. I told my friends that it was improper to expect an apology from the Superintendent unless he could be convinced that he was wrong. Their fast could carry no conviction to him of the wrongness of the punishment. Such conviction could be brought about only by reasoning. And, in any case, as *Satyagrahis* who were out for suffering, how could they fast against injustices whether done to them or their co-prisoners? My friends appreciated the force of my argument and Major Jones's generous statement did the rest. They agreed to break the fast and to persuade the others to do likewise. I asked for the Major's permission to give them a portion of my milk which he readily granted. They accepted the milk but said they would first take their bath and then take the milk in the company of the other hunger-strikers. The Major ordered milk and fruit diet for the strikers during the period of recuperation.

A hearty handshake between us all terminated the meeting. For the moment the officials were not officials and we were not prisoners. We were all friends engaged in solving a knotty problem and glad that it was solved. Thus ended this eventful hunger-strike. The Major admitted that this was the cleanest hunger strike he had witnessed. He had taken extraordinary precautions to see that no food was passed to the prisoners surreptitiously and he was satisfied that none was passed.

Had he known the stuff of which these strikers were made, he need not have taken any precautions at all.

One permanent result of the incident was that the Government passed orders that, except in cases of the gravest provocation and insult offered to the officials, flogging should not be administered without the previous sanction of the superior authority. The precaution was undoubtedly necessary. Whilst, in some matters, widest discretion must be given to the Superintendents of Jails, in matters such as punishments which cannot be recalled, the wisest of Superintendents must be subject to salutary checks.

There can be no doubt that the hunger-strike of Messrs Dastane and Dev and the other *Satyagrahis* produced startling results of a beneficial character. For the motive, though mistaken, was excellent and the action itself purely innocent. But though the result attained was good, the fast must be condemned. The good result was not a direct result of the fast but of repentance and admission of mistaken motive and consequent abandonment of the fast. Fasting by a *Satyagrahi* can only be justified when it is a shame to eat and live.

Thus, still confining my attention to a prisoner's conduct, it would be a shame to eat and live if I was deprived of religious liberty or degraded as a human being, as when food is thrown at me instead of being given to me in a courteous manner. It should be unnecessary to say that religious objection should be really so and discourtesy should be such as would be felt by an ordinary prisoner. The caution is necessary because a religious necessity is often pretended merely in order to embarrass, and discourtesy is often felt where none is meant.

I may not insist on keeping or bringing the *Bhagavad Gita* for the purpose of stealing in prohibited correspondence. I may not resent as discourtesy the ordinary search which every prisoner must undergo.

In *Satyagraha* there is no room for shams. But I would have been bound to fast, say, if the Government had not given me the opportunity of seeing the hunger-strikers merely with a view to understand their view-point and dissuade them from their error, if I found them to be erring. I could not afford to eat to live, when I knew that it was possible to prevent starvation if my keepers recognized the ordinary rules of humanity.

"But," say some friends, "why should you draw these fine distinctions? Why should we not embarrass the jail officials as we embarrass officials outside? Why should we co-operate as you co-operated with the jail authorities? Why should we not non-violently resist them? Why should we obey any regulations at all, save for our own convenience? Have we not a perfect right, is it not our duty, to paralyse the prison administration? If we make the officials' position uncomfortable without using any violence, the Government will find it difficult to arrest a large number and will thus be obliged to sue for peace." This argument has been seriously advanced. I must therefore, devote the next chapter to its consideration.

Young India, 22-5-1924

NOTES

1. Then secretary, Gujarat Provincial Congress Committee.
2. *Vide* "Letter to Jail Superintendent, Yeravda", 29-6-1923.

20
My Jail Experiences–VII

SATYAGRAHI PRISONERS' CONDUCT

The argument advanced by some friends and put by me at the end of the last chapter[1] deserves consideration if only because so many honestly believe in it and so many followed it out consistently in their conduct in 1921 and 1922, when thousands went to jail.

In the first instance, even outside the jails, embarrassment of the Government is not our Gaol. We are indifferent if the Government is embarrassed so long as our conduct is right. Our non-co-operation embarrasses the Government as nothing else can. But we non-co-operate as lawyers or Councillors because it is our duty. That is to say, we will not cease to non-co-operate if we discovered that our non-co-operation pleased the rulers. And we are so indifferent because we believe that, by non-co-operation, we must ultimately benefit ourselves.

But there cannot be any such non-co-operation in the jails. We do not enter them to serve a selfish end. We are taken there by the Government as criminals according so their estimation. Our business, therefore, is to disillusion them by acting in an exemplary (and by them expected) manner, just as our business outside is to disillusion them by avoiding, say, their law-courts, schools or Councils or titles and by showing that we are prepared to do without their doubtful benefits.

Whether all of us realize it or not the method of non-co-operation is a process of touching the heart and appealing to reason, not one of frightening by rowdyism. Rowdyism has no place in a non-violent movement.

I have often likened *Satyagrahi* prisoners to prisoners of war. Once caught by the enemy, prisoners of war act towards the enemy as friends. It will be considered dishonourable on the part of a soldier as a prisoner of war to deceive the enemy. It does not affect my argument that the Government does not regard *Satyagrahi* prisoners as prisoners of war. If we act as such, we shall soon command respect. We must make the prisons a neutral institution in which we may, nay, must co-operate to a certain extent.

We would be highly inconsistent and hardly self-respecting if, on the one hand, we deliberately break prison rules and, in the same breath, complain of punishment and strictness. We may not, for instance, resist and complain of search and, at the same time, conceal prohibited things in our blankets or our clothes. There is nothing in *Satyagraha* that I know whereby we may, under certain circumstances, tell untruths or practise other deception.

When we say that, if we make the lives of prison officials uncomfortable, the Government will be obliged to sue for peace, we either pay them a subtle compliment or regard them as simpletons. We pay a subtle compliment when we consider that, even though we may make prison officials' lives uncomfortable, the Government will look on in silence and hesitate to award us condign punishment so as utterly to break our spirit. That is to say, we regard the administrators to be so considerate and humane that they will not severely punish us even though we give them sufficient cause. As a matter of fact, they will not and do not hesitate to throw overboard all idea of decency and award not only authorized, but even unauthorized punishments on given occasions.

But it is my deliberate conviction that, had we but acted with uniform honesty and dignity behoving *Satyagrahis*, we should have disarmed all opposition on the part of the Government, and such strictly honourable behaviour on the part of so many prisoners would have at least shamed the Government into confessing their error in imprisoning so many honourable and innocent men. For, is it not their case that our non-violence is but a cloak for our violence? Do we not, therefore, play into their hands every time we are rowdy?

In my opinion, therefore, as *Satyagrahis* we are bound, when we become prisoners:

1. to act with the most scrupulous honesty;
2. to co-operate with the prison officials in their administration;
3. to set, by our obedience to all reasonable discipline, an example to co-prisoners;
4. to ask for no favours and claim no privileges which the meanest of prisoners do not get and which we do not need strictly for reasons of health;
5. not to fail to ask what we do so need and not to get irritated if we do not obtain it;
6. to do all the tasks allotted, to the utmost of our ability.

It is such conduct which will make the Government position uncomfortable and untenable. It is difficult for them to meet honesty with honesty for their want of faith and unpreparedness for such a rare eventuality. Rowdyism they expect and meet with a double dose of it.

They were able to deal with anarchical crime, but they have not yet found out any way of dealing with non-violence save by yielding to it.

The idea behind the imprisonment of a *Satyagrahi* is that he expects relief through humble submission to suffering. He believes that meek suffering for a just cause has a virtue all its own and infinitely greater than the virtue of the sword. This does not mean that we may not resist when the treatment touches our self-respect. Thus, for instance, we must resist to the point of death the use of abusive language by officials or if they were to throw our food at us which is often done. Insult and abuse are no part of an official's duty.

Therefore, we must resist them. But we may not resist search because it is part of prison regulations.

Nor are my remarks about mute suffering to be construed to mean that there should be no agitation against putting innocent prisoners like *Satyagrahis* in the same class as confirmed criminals. Only as prisoners we may not ask for favours. We must be content to live with the confirmed criminals and even welcome the opportunity of working moral reform in them. It is however expected of a Government that calls itself civilized to recognize the most natural divisions.

Young India, 5-6-1924

NOTE

1. *Vide* "My Jail Experiences-VI", 22-5-1924.

21
My Jail Experiences–VIII

JAIL ECONOMICS

Everyone who has any experience of jails knowbs that they are the most starved of all departments. The hospitals are comparatively the most expensive of public institutions. In the jails everything is of the simplest and the crudest type. In them there is extravagance in the spending of human labour, there is miserliness in the spending of money and materials. In hospitals it is just the reverse. And yet both are institutions designed tc deal with human diseases—jails for mental and hospitals for physical. Mental diseases are regarded as a crime and therefore punishable; physical diseases are regarded as unforeseen visitations of nature to be indulgently treated. As a matter of fact, there is no reason for any such distinction. Mental as well as physical diseases are traceable to the same causes. If I steal, I commit a breach of laws governing healthy society. If I suffer from stomach-ache, I still commit a breach of laws governing a healthy society. One reason why physical diseases are treated lightly is because the so-called higher classes break the laws of physical health—perhaps more frequently than the lower classes. The higher classes have no occasion for committing crude thefts and, as their lives would be disturbed if thefts continued, they being generally law-givers, polish gross stealing, knowing all the while that their swindles which pass muster are far more harmful to society than the crude thefts. It is curious, too, that both institutions flourish because of wrong treatment. Hospitals flourish because patients are indulged and humoured, jails flourish because the prisoners are punished as if they were beyond recall. If every disease, mental or physical, were regarded as a lapse, but every patient or prisoner were to be treated kindly and sympathetically, not severely or indulgently, both jails and hospitals would show a tendency to decrease. A hospital no more than a jail is a necessity for a healthy society. Every patient and every prisoner should come out of his hospital or jail as a missionary to preach the gospel of mental and physical health.

But I must stop the comparison at this stage. The reader will be surprised to learn that the parsimony in prisons is exercised on the ground of economy. Although all labour is taken from prisoners, e.g., drawing water, grinding flour, cleaning roads and closets, cooking food, the prisoners are not only not self-supporting, but they do not even pay for their own food. And in spite of all their labour, the prisoners do not get the food they would like nor the manner of cooking they would appreciate; this for the simple reason that the prisoners who do the cooking, etc., are not as a rule interested in their work. It is for them a task to be performed under unsympathetic supervision. It is easy enough to see that, if the prisoners were philanthropists and, therefore, felt interested in the welfare of their fellow prisoners, they would not find themselves in prisons. If, therefore, a more rational and more moral system of administration was adopted, the prisons would easily become self-supporting reformatories instead of, as they are now, expensive penal settlements. I would save the terrible waste of labour in drawing water, grinding flour, etc. If I was incharge, I would buy flour from outside, I would draw water by machinery and, instead of having all kinds of odd jobs, I would devote the prisons to agriculture, hand-spinning and hand-weaving. In the small jails only spinning and weaving may be kept. Even now weaving there is in most of the central prisons. All that is necessary is to add carding and hand-spinning. All the cotton needed can be easily grown in connection with many jails.[*sic*] This will popularize the national cottage industry and make the prisons self-supporting. The labour of all the prisoners will be utilized for remunerative and yet not for competitive purposes, as is now the case in some respects. There is a printing press attached to the Yeravda Jail. Now this press is largely worked by convict labour. I regard this as unfair competition with the general printing presses. If the prisons were to run competitive industries, they would easily be made even profitable. But my purpose is to show that they can be made self-supporting without entering into such competition and, at the same time, teach the inmates a home industry which on their discharge would give them an independent calling, thus providing for them every incentive to live as respectable citizens.

I would moreover provide for the prisoners as homely an atmosphere as is consistent with public safety. I would thus give them all facility for seeing their relatives, getting books and even tuition. I would replace distrust by reasonable trust. I would credit them with every bit of work they might do and let them buy their own food, cooked or raw.

I would make most of the sentences indeterminate, so that a prisoner will not be detained a moment longer than is necessary for the protection of society and for his own reform.

I know that this requires a thorough reorganization and the employing of a different kind of warders from the ex-military men that most of them are now. But I know, too, that the reform can be initiated without much extra cost.

At the present moment, the prisons are rest-houses for rogues and torture-houses for ordinary simple prisoners which the majority are. The rogues manage to get all they want, the simple untutored prisoners do not get even what they need. Under the scheme which I have endeavoured to sketch in its barest outline, the rogues will have to be straight before they feel comfortable, and the simple innocent prisoners will have as favourable an atmosphere as is possible to give them in the circumstances. Honesty will be remunerative and dishonesty at a discount.

By making the prisoners pay for their food in work, there will be little idleness. And by having only agriculture and cotton manufacture, including what handicrafts may be required for these two industries, the expensive supervision will be considerably lessened.

Young India, 12-6-1924

22
My Jail Experiences–IX

SOME CONVICT-WARDERS

I have already dealt with the system of appointing convicts as officers or warders. I hold the system to be thoroughly bad and demoralizing.

The prison officials know it. They say it is due to economy.

They think that the jails cannot be efficiently administered with the present paid staff without supplementing it with convict-officers.

There is no doubt that, unless the reform suggested by me in the last chapter is inaugurated, it is not possible to do away with the system of entrusting convicts with responsible duties without a very large increase in the prison expenditure.

However, it is not my purpose in this chapter to deal any further with prison reform. I simply wish to relate my happy experiences of the convict officers who were appointed to watch over and look after us.

When Mr. Banker and I were transferred to the Yeravda Central Prison, there was one warder and one *bardasi*. The latter is what the name implies, a mere servant. The convict warder whose acquaintance we first made was a Hindu from the Punjab side. His name was Harkaran. He was convicted of murder. The murder according to him was not premeditated but due to a fit of anger. By occupation he was a petty merchant. His sentence was fourteen years, of which he had almost served nine years. He was fairly old. The prison life had told on him. He was always brooding and most anxious to be discharged.

He was therefore, morose and peevish. He was conscious of his high dignity. He was patronizing to those who obeyed and served him. He bullied those who crossed his path. To look at him, no one would think he could be guilty of murder. He could read Urdu fluently. He was religiously minded and was fond of reading *bhajans* in Urdu. The Yeravda library has a few books for prisoners in several Indian languages, e.g., Hindi, Urdu, Marathi, Gujarati, Sindhi, Canarese, Tamil. Harkaran was not above keeping and hiding trifles in defiance of jail regulations. He was in the majority. It would be regarded snobbish and foolish not to steal trifles. A prisoner who did not follow this unwritten law would have a bad time of it from his fellows.

Ostracism would be the least punishment. If the whole of the jail yard were to be dug up twelve inches deep, it would yield up many a secret in the shape of spoons, knives, pots, cigarettes, soap and such like.

Harkaran, being one of the oldest inmates of Yeravda, was a sort of purveyor-general to the prisoners. If a prisoner wanted anything Harkaran was the supplier. I wanted a knife for cutting my bread and lemons. Harkaran could procure it if I would have it through him. If I wanted to go through the elaborate process of asking the Superintendent, that was my business. I must be prepared for a snubbing. When we became friends, he related all his wonderful exploits; how he dodged officials, how he procured for himself and others dainties, what skilful tricks were employed by prisoners to obtain what they wanted and how it was almost impossible (in his opinion) not to resort to these tricks, was described in minute detail and with much gusto. He was horrified to discover that I was neither interested in the exploits nor was I minded to join the trade. He endeavoured subsequently somewhat to repair the indiscretion he had let himself into, and to assure me that he had seen my point and that he would thenceforth refrain from the irregularities. But I have a suspicion that the repentance was put on. The reader, however, must not run away with the idea that the jail officials do not know these irregularities. They are all an open secret. They not only know them, but often sympathize with the prisoners who do these tricks to make themselves happy and comfortable. They (the officials) believe in the doctrine of 'live and let live'. A prisoner, who behaves correctly in the presence of his superiors, obeys their orders, does not quarrel with his fellows and does not inconvenience officials, is practically free to break any regulation for the sake of procuring greater comfort.

Well, the first acquaintance with Harkaran was not particularly happy. He knew that we were 'important' prisoners. But so was he in a way. After all, he was an officer with a long and honourable record of service behind him. He was no respecter of persons Mr. Banker was torn away from me the very next morning. Harkaran allowed the full force of his authority to descend upon me. I was not to do this or that I was not to cross the white line referred to in my letter to Hakimji.

But I had not the faintest idea of retaliating or resenting what he said or did. I was too engrossed in my own work and studies even to think of Harkaran's simple and childish instructions. It gave me momentary amusement. Harkaran discovered his error. When he saw that I did not resent his officiousness, nor did I pay any attention to it, he felt nonplussed.

He was unprepared for such an emergency. He, therefore, took the only course that was left open to him and that was to recognize my dissimilarity and respond to me when I refused to respond to him. My non-violent non-co-operation led to his co-operation. All non-violent non-co-operation, whether among individuals or societies, or whether between governments and the governed, must lead ultimately to hearty co-operation. Anyway Harkaran and I became perfect friends. When Mr. Banker was returned to me, he put the finishing touch. One of his many businesses in the jail was to boom me for all I was worth. He thought that Harkaran and others had not sufficiently realized my greatness. In two or three days time I found myself elevated to the position of a baby in woollens. I was too great to be allowed to sweep my own cell or to put out my own blankets for drying. Harkaran was all attention before, but now he became embarrassingly attentive. I could not do anything myself, not even wash a handkerchief. If Harkaran heard me washing it, he would enter the open bath-room and tear the kerchief away from me. Whether it was that the authorities suspected that Harkaran was doing anything unlawful for us or whether it was a mere accident, Harkaran was, to our sorrow, taken away from us. He felt the separation more perhaps than we did. He had a royal time with us. He had plenty of eatables and that openly from our rations, supplemented as they were with fruit that friends sent from outside. And as our fame was 'noised abroad', Harkaran's association with us had given him an added status with the other prisoners.

When I was given the permission to sleep on the cell verandah, the authorities thought that it was too risky to leave me with one warder only. Probably, the regulations required that a prisoner whose cell was kept open should have two warders to watch over him. It might even be that the addition was made for my protection. Whatever, the cause, another warder was posted for night duty. His name was Shabaskhan. I never inquired about the cause, but I thought that a Mohammedan was chosen to balance the Hindu Harkaran. Shabaskhan was a powerful Baloochi. He was Harkaran's contemporary.

Both knew each other well. Shabaskhan too was convicted of murder. It resulted from an affray in the clan to which he belonged. Shabaskhan was as broad as he was tall. His build always reminded me of Shaukat Ali. Shabaskhan put me at ease the very first day. He said, 'I am not going to watch you at all. Treat me as your friend and do exactly as you like. You will never find me interfering with you. If you want anything done, I shall be only too happy if I can do it for you. Shabaskhan was as good as his word. He was always Polite. He often tempted me with prison delicacies and always felt genuinely sorry that I would not partake of them. 'You know,' he would say, "if we do not help ourselves to these few things, life would be intolerable, eating the same things day in and day out. With your people, it is different. You come for religion. That fact sustains you, whereas we know that we have committed crimes. We would like to get away as soon as ever we can." Shabaskhan was the jailor's favourite. Growing enthusiastic over him, he once said, 'Look at him. I consider him to be a perfect gentleman. In a fit of temper he has committed murder for which he truly repents. I assure you there are not many men outside who are better than Shabaskhan. It is a mistake to suppose that all prisoners are criminals. Shabaskhan I have found to be most trustworthy and courteous. If I had the power, I would discharge him today. The jailor was not wrong. Shabaskhan was a good man, and he was by no means the only good prisoner in that jail. Let me note in passing that it was not the jail that had made him good. He was good outside.

It is customary in the jails never to keep a convict officer on the same duty for any length of time. Transfers constantly take place. It is a necessary precaution Prisoners cannot be allowed, under the existing system, to develop intimate relations. We had, therefore, a most varied experience of convict officers. After about two months, Shabaskhan was replaced by Adan. But I must introduce this warder to the reader in the next chapter.

Young India, 26-6-1924

23
My Jail Experiences–X

SOME CONVICT-WARDERS

Adan was a young Somali soldier who was sentenced to ten years' hard labour for desertion from the British Army, which he had joined during the War. He was transferred by the Aden Jail authorities.

Adan had served four years when we were admitted. He was practically illiterate. He could read the *Quran* with difficulty, but could not copy it correctly, if at all. He was able to speak Urdu fairly fluently and was anxious to learn Urdu. With the permission of the Superintendent, I tried to teach him, but the learning of the alphabet proved too great a strain upon him and he left it. With all that he was quick-witted and sharp as a needle. He took the greatest interest in religious matters. He was a devout Mussalman, offered his prayers regularly including the midnight one, and never missed the *Ramzan* fast. The rosary was his constant companion. When he was free, he used to recite selections from the *Quran*. He would often engage me in a discussion on complete fasts according to the Hindu custom as also on *ahimsa*. He was a brave man. He was very courteous, but never cringing. He was of an excitable nature and, therefore, often quarrelled with the *bardasi* or his fellow-warder. We had, therefore. sometimes to arbitrate between them. Being a soldier and amenable to reason, he would accept the award, but he would put his case boldly and cogently. Adan was the longest with us. I treasure Adan's affection. He was most attentive to me. He would see to it that I got my food at the appointed time.

He was sad if I ever became ill and anticipated all my wants. He would not let me exert myself for anything. He was anxious to be discharged or at least to be transferred to Aden. I tried hard. I drew up petitions[1] for him. The Superintendent too, tried his best. But the decision rested with the Aden authorities. Hope was held out to him that he would be discharged before the end of last year. I do hope he is already discharged. The little service I rendered gave rise to deep personal attachment. It was a sad parting when Adan was transferred to another part of the prison. I must not omit to mention that, when I was organizing spinning and carding in the jail, Adan, though one of his hands was disabled, helped most industriously at making slivers. He became very proficient in the art which he had come to like.

As Shabaskhan was replaced by Adan, Harkaran was replaced by Bhiwa. Much to our agreeable surprise, Bhiwa was a Mahar from Maharashtra and, therefore, an untouchable. Of all the warders we met he was perhaps the most industrious. The reader will be surprised to find that the canker of untouchability has not left even the jails untouched. Poor Bhiwa! He would not enter our cells without considerable hesitation. He would not touch our pots. We quickly set him at rest by telling him that we had not only no prejudices against untouchables, but that we were trying our best to do away with the curse. Shankerlal Banker specially befriended him and made him feel perfectly at home with us. He permitted Bhiwa to be so familiar with him that the former would resent an angry word from Mr. Banker and the latter would even apologize. He induced Bhiwa to apply himself to studies and taught him also spinning. The result was that Bhiwa became, in an incredibly short space of time, an accomplished spinner and began so to like it that he thought of learning weaving, and earning his living through that occupation when he went out. I cultivated in the jail the habit of drinking hot water and lemon at 4.15 a.m. When I protested against Mr. Banker doing it for me, he initiated Bhiwa into the mystery. Prisoners, though they get up early enough, do not like to leave their matting (which is their bed) at that early hour. Bhiwa, however, immediately responded to his friend's suggestion.

But it was Mr. Banker's business always to wake up Bhiwa at 4 O'clock. When Bhiwa went (he was discharged under special remission), Adan undertook the duty. He will not listen to my doing it myself. And the tradition was kept up even after Mr. Tanker's discharge, each outgoing warder initiating the incoming one into all the mysteries. Needless to say, this morning duty was no part of the prison task. Indeed, convicts when they became warders were not expected to do any labour at all. Theirs is but to order.

Even as the best of friends must part some day, Bhiwa bade good-bye. He was permitted to receive from Mr. Banker *khaddar* caps, *khaddar dhotis*, *khaddar* vests and a *khaddar* blanket. He promised to wear nothing but *khaddar* outside. Let me hope good Bhiwa, wherever he may be, is keeping the promise.

Bhiwa was followed by Thamu. He too belonged to Maharashtra. Thamu was a mild-mannered warder. He had not much 'go' in him. He would do what he was asked, but did not believe in specially exerting himself. He and Adan, therefore, did not get on quite well together. But Thamu, being timid, always yielded to Adan in the end.

He had such a royal time (all had) with us that Thamu did not want to be separated from us. He, therefore, preferred to bear Adan's hard yoke to being transferred. Thamu having come to us a considerable time after Adan, the latter was Thamu's senior with us. It is remarkable how these fictitious seniorities spring up in little places like jails.

Yeravda was to us a whole world or, better still, the whole world. Every squabble, every little jar, was a mighty event commanding sustained interest for the day and sometimes even for days. If the jail authorities permitted a jail newspaper to be conducted by the prisoners and for them, it would have a cent per cent circulation, and such toothsome news as properly-cooked dhal, well-dressed vegetables, and sensational items as war of words between prisoners, sometimes even resulting in blows and consequent *khatla* (trial) before the Superintendent, would be as eagerly devoured by the prisoners as the news of big dinner parties and great wars are devoured by the public outside. I make the present of a suggestion to enterprising members of the Assembly that, if they desire fame, they cannot do better than introduce a bill requiring Superintendents of jails to permit the publishing and editing of newspapers by prisoners exclusively for their own use and under strict censorship by the authorities.

To return to Thamu, though he was flabby, as a man he was otherwise as good as any of his predecessors. He took to the *charkha* like fish to water. In a week's time, he pulled a more even thread than I did. And after a month, the pupil out-distanced the teacher by a long way. So much so that I grew jealous of Thamu's superiority. I saw too from Thamu's rapid progress that my slow progress was a peculiar defect of mine and that an ordinary person could pull a perfect thread in a month at the outside. Everyone of those who were taught by me excited me in no time. To Thamu as to Bhiwa, the spinning-wheel had become a welcome companion. They were able to drown the sorrows of separation from their nearest in the soft and gentle music of the wheel. Later on, spinning became Thamu's first work in the morning. He span at the rate of four hours per day.

When we were shifted to the European yard, there were several changes. Among them was a change of warders. Adan was the first to be transferred. Though neither he nor we liked it, we took his transfer bravely. Then came Thamu's turn. Poor fellow, he broke down. He wanted me to try to keep him. I would not do that. I thought it was beyond my province. The authorities had a perfect right to shift whom and where they would. Adan and Thamu were followed by Kunti, a Gurkha, and a Canarese by name Gangappa. The Gurkha was called Goorkha by everybody. He was reserved, but grew 'chummy' later on. For the first few days, he did not know where he was.

Probably he thought we would report and involve him on the slightest pretext. But when he saw that we meant no mischief, he came closer to us. But he was soon transferred. Gangappa I have partly described in the introduction to the jail correspondence. He was an elderly man.

His almost punctilious observance of rules and his great devotion to duty commanded my admiration. He put his whole soul into whatever he was ordered by the authorities to do. He took up duties which he need not have. He rarely remained idle. He learnt to make and cook *chapatis* for my companions. His devotion to me personally I shall never forget. No wife or sister could be more unsparing than Gangappa in his attention. He was awake at all times. He took delight in anticipating my wants. He saw to it that all my things were kept spotlessly clean. During my illness, he was my most efficient nurse, because he was the most attentive. When we were transferred to the European yard, Messrs Mansar Ali and Yagnik used to join me at prayer time. Mr. Mansar Ali was transferred to Allahabad for his discharge in due course. Mr. Yagnik, because he needed more intensive and philosophical rather than devotional meditation, dropped out.

Gangappa felt that without these friends I would feel lonely at prayer. The very first time that he saw that I was alone at prayer, he quietly took his seat in front of me. Needless to say, I appreciated the delicate courtesy underlying the action. It was so spontaneous, unofficious, and natural for Gangappa I do not call it religious in the accepted sense of the term, though, according to my conception, it was truly religious. I always hesitate to invite anybody to these prayer meetings of mine. I did not want them to come for my sake. I did not feel lonely. I realized most at that time the companionship of God. If any one came, I wanted him not for keeping company but for sharing the divine companionship. I, therefore, particularly hesitated to invite the warders. I felt they might join merely out of form, whereas I wanted them to join only if they naturally felt like joining. With Gangappa it was a mixture of pity for me in my loneliness and desire to share with me the sacred half-hour, though he could understand not a word of what I sang save, of course, *Ramanam*. Gangappa drew to the prayer meeting another warder, Annappa, also a Canarese, and later, Ms Abdul Gani felt impelled to join. I imagine that Mr. Abdul Gani was unconsciously influenced by Gangappa's unobtrusive act of joining me.

The reader will see that I had a uniformly happy experience of these convict-warders. I could not have wished for more devoted companions or more faithful attendants. Paid service would but be a patch upon this and that of friends could only equal it. And yet the pity of it is that society treats such men as criminals and outcastes because they had the misfortune to be convicted. I entirely endorse the remark of the Head Jailor, already quoted by me in a previous chapter 1, that there are in our jails many men who are better than those outside. The reader will now understand why I felt a pang when I heard that I was discharged, and most of the companions who had covered me with so much kindness and whom there was, in my opinion, no occasion to detain any longer in the jails were left behind.

One word more and I must regretfully part with Gangappa. Gangappa always knew his limitations. He would not spin. He said he could not do it. His fingers had not the cunning for it. But he kept the work-room in order, cleaned my wheel and devoted all his spare time to sunning and cleaning the cotton for carding.

Of all the many happy memories of my prison life, I know that those of the company of the convict-warders will perhaps linger the longest.

Young India, 10-7-1924

NOTE

1. These are not available.

Appendices

Appendix–I
Who Can Go To Gaol?

Last week we briefly considered the question: Who can be a *Satyagrahi*? In the Transvaal, *Satyagraha* consists for the most part in going to gaol. But imprisonment is not the end of the matter.

Satyagrahis have had to mount the gallows,[1] embrace a pillar of red hot iron[2], suffer being rolled down a mountain, swim in boiling oil in a big frying pan,[3] walk through a blazing forest[4], suffer loss of a kingdom and be sold [as slave] in a low-born family[5] and stay in a lion's den. Thus, *Satyagrahis* have had to pass through different ordeals in different parts of the world.

In the Transvaal, the ordeal for the *Satyagrahis* consists merely in going to gaol. Hence, it will be useful to inquire as to who can go to gaol. Some Indians were willing to go to gaol, but did not do so—could not do so—owing to one reason or another. What could have been those reasons? This question will answer itself it we find out who can go to gaol.

Every person, then, who wants to go to gaol must have, in some measure, the qualities which, as we have seen, are essential in a *Satyagrahi*. But, in addition, he should have the following strong points:

(1) Freedom from addiction to harmful things.
(2) A well-disciplined body.
(3) Disregard for comfortable seat or bed.
(4) Extreme simplicity in food habits.

(5) Total freedom from false sense of prestige or status.
(6) Fortitude.

Friends who would go to gaol must particularly have these qualities (which we may call the six forms of wealth in a prison.). Let us examine each of them. It was our experience that those prisoners who were addicted to smoking, drinking, betel-nuts or even tea found the strain of gaol life too much. In consequence, they either managed to get these things surreptitiously in gaol, that is, abandoned [the path of] truth, or gave up speaking of going to gaol again. One must therefore avoid every form of addiction. One addiction alone is permissible, and that is repeating the name of the Lord in prayer.

Cowards can never become *Satyagrahis*. Likewise, a physical wreck will not generally be able to bear gaol life. There have been many cases of men who, though physically weak, have braved hardships through sheer will-power. These are exceptions. As a general rule, one must have a healthy and sound constitution; lacking this, some of the prisoners were unable to bear the strain [of gaol-life].

A *Satyagrahi* knows that his body is [as it were] lent to him on hire. He should prove a worthy tenant by keeping it clean and glowing with health.

One can understand that a man who is accustomed to a spring cot with a soft mattress cannot all at once bring himself to sleep on the floor. One must therefore get rid of this pampering of the body.

Diet, it seems, has proved to be much the most important problem. That also is not surprising. He who has his tongue under control, being both sparing in speech and moderate in his taste for good food, must be reckoned to have achieved a great conquest. We hardly come across anyone who does not relish good food. Even the poor Kaffirs die with craving for good food. Of course, this is not a simple problem. However, those who want to offer themselves for imprisonment in a public cause must learn to master their palate. The proper thing is to offer thanks to God for whatever we get. Every Indian must ponder over the fact that, in India, thirty million out of a population of three hundred million get only one meal a day, and that, too, nothing more than *roti* and salt. Compared to this, it is not much of a hardship to have to maintain oneself in gaol on three meals a day, each different from the other. Hunger accepts everything.

Though one may not feel at ease for a few days, by and by one does come to like gaol food. Any Indian who wants to be a *Satyagrahi*—a prisoner—must accustom himself to simple food as quickly as possible.

A person with a false notion of prestige or status cannot afford to go to gaol. One is subjected there to the authority of the warder and is asked to do work which is thought rather degrading. If one refuses to do such work, considering it dishonourable, or on the ground that one has never done it before, the result will be unwelcome. Whether on thinks of anything as a mark of servitude or not depends entirely on one's mind. He who is free in his mind will feel as free as a king even when carrying buckets [of night-soil]. Rather than feel that carrying of buckets is a mark of servitude, such a man will consider it a matter of honour in the present circumstances.

And last, Lady Fortitude. Everyone starts counting days the moment he is in gaol, with the result that they appear to grow inordinately long. Years wore on while we were outside and were lost to us forever. And yet we did not think much of that. In gaol, three days appeared to be as long as three years. Why? The answer is that we were not happy to be in gaol. Just as a mother takes pleasure in suffering for the sake of the child, so also must we take pleasure in suffering for the motherland—for truth. One must patiently serve out the full term of one's imprisonment, bearing always in mind that one could never have passed one's days outside in the same manner as in gaol and put the time to good use, that is, spent the days in devotion to God, in good thoughts, in self-examination. In this way, going along a single path one will have accomplished two tasks.

These six qualities, therefore, a [*Satyagrahi*] prisoner must have. There may be other qualities which will suggest themselves to the reader. But we urge every reader to ponder, at any rate, the suggestions made above.

[From Gujarati]

Indian Opinion, 5-6-1909

NOTES

1. The reference probably is to the crucifixion of Jesus.
2. These are references to legends of Prahlad, Sudhanva, Nala-Damayanti and Harishchandra, respectively.
3. *Ibid.*
4. *Ibid.*
5. *Ibid.*

Appendix–II
Gandhi's Imprisonments

TOTAL IMPRISONMENT

Total Imprisonment Awarded: Twelve years, two months, six days.

Total Simple Imprisonment Awarded: Eleven years, three months, six days.

Total Rigorous Imprisonment Awarded: Eleven months.

Total Actual Imprisonment: Six years, four months, twenty-four days.

Total Actual Simple Imprisonment: Six years, one month, sixteen days.

Total Actual Rigorous Imprisonment: Three months, and eight days.

Total Actual Rigorous Imprisonment in South Africa: Seven months and eight days.

Total Actual Imprisonment in India: Five years; nine months and sixteen days.

Details of the Imprisonment

1. Johannesburg Imprisonment

Method of courting imprisonment: By disobeying the orders to leave the colony within the prescribed time-limit.

Imprisonment awarded: Two months' simple imprisonment.

Actual duration of imprisonment: Twenty-days simple imprisonment (January 10 to January 30, 1908).

Ground of Release: In view of the Gandhi-Smuts Agreement regarding the voluntary registration and its validation.

2. Volksrust Imprisonment

Method of courting imprisonment: By entering Transvaal without registration certificates and by refusing to give his finger and thumb impressions.

Imprisonment awarded: Seven days simple and two months rigorous imprisonment.

Actual duration of imprisonment: Seven-days simple and two months rigorous imprisonment. (October 7 to October 14, 1908) and (October 14 to December12, 1908).

Ground of release: Completion of the awarded imprisonment.

3. Valksrust-Pretoria Imprisonment

Method of courting imprisonment: By entering Transvaal without registration certificates and by refusing to give his finger and thumb impressions.

Imprisonment awarded: Three months simple imprisonment Actual duration of imprisonment. Three months' simple imprisonment (February 25 to May 24, 1909).

Ground of release: Completion of the awarded imprisonment.

4. Palmford-Valksrust Imprisonment

Method of courting imprisonment: By inducing strike of Ballengeich Indian miners and Ladysmith Railway men and by taking them to stage a march from Naw Castle to the Transvaal without requisite registration certificates to protest against f-3 tax.

Imprisonment awarded: Nine months' rigorous imprisonment.

Actual duration of imprisonment: One month and eight days rigorous and three days simple imprisonment (November 6, 9, 10, 1913 and November 11 to December 18, 1913).

Ground of Release: Recommendations of the Solomon Commission.

5. I-Yervada Imprisonment

Method of courting imprisonment: By writing four articles in his Young India, amounting in the Government's opinion to sedition.

Imprisonment awarded: Six years' simple imprisonment. Actual duration of imprisonment: One year, ten months and twenty-seven day's simple imprisonment (March 10 to March 17, 1922 and March 18, 1922 to February 5, 1924).

Ground of Release: In view of the seriousness of his health.

6. II-Yervada Imprisonment

Method of courting imprisonment: By violating salt laws at Dandi and by asking others to do the same for achieving *Purna Swaraj* or complete independence for India.

Imprisonment awarded: During Government's pleasure actual duration of imprisonment: Eight month's and twenty-two days' simple imprisonment (May 4, 1930 to January 25, 1931).

Ground of Release: In the "hope of restoration of peaceful conditions."

7. III-Yervada Imprisonment

Method of courting imprisonment: By dispatching to the Viceroy an ultimatum to review civil disobedience movement of the attainment of *Purna Swaraj* for India.

Imprisonment awarded: During Government's pleasure. Actual duration of imprisonment: One year, four months and five days (January 4, 1932, to May 8, 1933).

Ground of Release: "In view of the nature and object of the fast" Gandhi imposed on himself on this day.

8. IV-Yervada Imprisonment

Method of courting imprisonment: By continuing and intensifying the civil disobedience movement for the attainment of *Purna Swaraj* for India.

Imprisonment awarded: During Government's pleasure. Actual duration of imprisonment: Three days (August 1 to August 4, 1933).

Ground of Release: After being served with a restraint order requiring him to reside within the limits of Poona City.

9. V-Yervada Imprisonment

Method of courting imprisonment: By disobeying the restraint orders requiring him to reside within the limits of the Poona city.

Imprisonment awarded: One year simple imprisonment. Actual duration of imprisonment: Twenty days simple imprisonment (August 4 to August 23, 1933).

Ground of Release: When he was considered to have entered the danger zone, he was released unconditionally (on medical grounds).

10. Aga Khan Palace Imprisonment

Method of courting imprisonment: Although this time Gandhi did not want court imprisonment, the Government, by precipitating the inauguration of Quit India Movement,—arrested and detained him under the Defence India Rules.

Imprisonment awarded: During Government's pleasure. Actual duration of imprisonment: One year, eight months and twenty-nine days. (August 9, 1942 to May 6, 1944).

Ground of Release: His anaemic condition had worsened and blood-pressure fallen.

Index